PENGU

PC

André Launay was born in London in 1930 of French parentage. Educated at Lancing, he went to France to learn about the food trade before joining an old established London firm manufacturing and importing luxury foods, of which he is now a director. In 1954 he married a well-known fashion model and published a book of cartoons, *I Married a Model*, on the *haute couture* world. This led him to write for radio and television. In 1956 his play *A Man on the Balcony* won an award at the Cheltenham Festival of Contemporary Literature and in 1958 *The Aimless* was produced at the Edinburgh Festival. Living at Halse, in Somerset, with his wife and two young sons, he has since published six crime novels, broadcasts frequently from the West Country and writes works of fiction and non-fiction.

ANDRÉ LAUNAY

POSH FOOD

with drawings by
Carol Barker

PENGUIN BOOKS

Penguin Books Ltd, Harmondsworth, Middlesex, England
Penguin Books Inc., 3300 Clipper Mill Road, Baltimore 11, Md, U.S.A
Penguin Books Australia Ltd, Ringwood, Victoria, Australia

—

First published as *Caviare and After* by Macdonald 1964
Published in Penguin Handbooks 1967
Copyright © André Launay, 1964

—

Made and printed in Great Britain
by Cox & Wyman Ltd,
London, Reading and Fakenham
Set in Monotype Garamond

CONTENTS

FOREWORD

THIS entertaining and witty guide to the plush mysteries of luxury eating not only makes amusing reading for someone like myself (although I think I can claim with justice to know my way around most menus by this time!), but will undoubtedly prove extremely useful to all young people blessed with an awakening palate, a quickening interest in good food, and the financial means to gratify their curiosity. I have no hesitation in saying that it is a *good thing* for people to take an interest in cultivating their taste for the luxuries of life, above all food, be they budding executives with expense accounts or ambitious young men and women who are earning a fair amount of money by their own exertions and are seeking, quite rightly, to reap their just rewards, including the gastronomic ones. Gather ye rosebuds while ye may – and while your livers and ulcers permit!

London, 1964.

BOOTHBY

ACKNOWLEDGEMENTS

I would like to thank Mr Gordon Cridlan, Mr Robert Worne and the Staff of Messrs V. Benoist Ltd, for all the help they have given me in getting the facts for this book. Also Monsieur Hubert Bijon of Messrs F. Feyel, Strasbourg, Monsieur Alain Pebeyre of Messrs P. Pebeyre, Cahors, Messrs Jacques Fuche of Nice, Mr Joseph Barnett of Barnetts of Frying Pan Alley, Messrs W. G. White Ltd, Mr Victor Brusa of the White Elephant Club, London, Mrs Dorothy Grafton, Monsieur and Madame Roger Brines for allowing me access to their rare and comprehensive library of gastronomic books and last, but not least, my father.

INTRODUCTION

I WAS eight when I attended my first banquet. It was at Frascati's, a restaurant that played a major part in the life of Oxford Street, but is now, alas, only a fond memory.

The occasion was the reunion of the French colony domiciled in London, and my father, who was not only a Frenchman but also a leading light in the field of gastronomics, obviously had some say in the composition of the menu; for most of what we ate seemed to be supplied by the firm of comestible importers he then admirably managed.

Frascati's, if I remember rightly, was at the time very gold with tall balustrades and vast staircases, enormous waiters and even more enormous chefs.

Our party was comprised of relations, all connoisseurs *par excellence* of fine foods and all somehow involved in contributing to the magnificent fare we were there to digest.

One of my godfathers, I believe, had been responsible for the shooting of some three hundred grouse, another godfather for fishing out the salmon, each had had a splendid holiday in Scotland.

The dinner began by an unassuming stone pot, buried deep in broken ice in the centre of a silver platter, being placed in the middle of the table, accompanied by the reverential gasps of all present.

When the stone lid was removed from the pot, more gasps followed at the sight of what seemed to me to be a mass of glutinous twelve-bore shot.

The glutinous mess was, of course, nothing less than caviare, and everyone went completely berserk.

It tasted delicious. On very thin buttered toast, but with nothing else, I had my fill, and was very thankful that someone had managed to persuade my parents that the education of the human palate started at an early age.

After caviare there followed soup. I can't really remember what it was, but it had sherry in it and the surrounding gold pillars and balustrades became pleasantly blurred.

Two slices of *foie gras* followed, during the savouring of which it was explained to me that the idea of the banquet was to over-indulge, as never before. There were rumours of war and the colony was determined to make the most of it while it could, so that for years after they would have a 'meal to remember'.

With the caviare, the soup and the *foie gras*, wine was poured out in liberal doses. I was sitting next to a huge uncle. He had a fierce beard and a monocle with an eye behind it. The latter disapprovingly fastened on to my thin arms and hollow cheeks and threatened me with certain damnation if I didn't 'eat up!' I swallowed everything I was given and by the time we got to the *Poularde Truffée à la Périgourdine*, I had to be excused.

I was ill for days afterwards and everyone was very distressed, not for me, but for my constitution. If I was to be a good representative of the family business it would hardly do for me to pass out every time I had a few tasty morsels.

Such a banquet, however, was never to be repeated, for war was indeed declared and after that I was brought up religiously on British Restaurant stodge, rather dubious fish caught in the local river and dandelion salad.

At the tender age of seventeen, in 1947, I was taken for my first post-war holiday abroad and, on the banks of Lake Geneva, faced my first four-course lunch for ten years. *Artichauts à la Grecque, Truite de Rivière à l'Hôtelière, Coq au Vin*, and *Soufflé Ambassadrice*, with a bottle of Rosé d'Anjou.

This excellent little meal, I realized later, was cunningly calculated to re-awaken my taste for good food. I was still at school but had to decide on a career – and whether it was the *Coq au Vin* or the brandy that followed that swayed me, I do not know. At any rate, I decided, as my father had hoped, to join him in manufacturing and importing high-class table delicacies – with beautiful thoughts of spending days sitting at a table sampling Quail in Aspic, Larks' Tongues and the occasional Derby Round of Beef.

My first job as an apprentice was in a slaughter-house in the south-west of France, a period on which I would rather not dwell. After that I spent several years in various very hot kitchens to emerge, eventually, reasonably well informed about *la cuisine française* and all its attendant virtues.

Paying frequent visits to restaurants of high repute then became a pleasant pastime and I discovered that I had one great advantage over my contemporaries. I always knew what I was eating.

Whereas one or two of my friends could discuss the merits of a Pontet-Canet or guess the vintage of a Château-Lafite, I had absolutely no one with whom to argue about the quality of some *Escargots Comtesse Riguidi* or *Pâté Chaud de Bécassines Lucullus*.

It is a strange fact that people who really enjoy a meal get even more pleasure out of it by discussing a *Sole Meunière* while eating *Canard à l'Orange* or criticizing a Pont l'Évêque they had two years ago while sampling a Brie.

It has also come to my notice that if you make it clear to a waiter that you know exactly what a *Pâté de Volaille* is, and that if it comes out as veal and ham pie you have every right to complain, you will get a far better portion next time and he will genuinely remember you without expecting a large tip. To know is, after all, to be respected, as someone must have said.

In the pages that follow I have set down the various facts I have learned and gathered during my years in the food trade, and notes about the delicacies and luxury items which are generally regarded as the most important on a menu.

This book has no recipes.

Housewives will not be able to prop it up against the cooker and dash off a *Potage Velouté de Grenouilles à la Sicilienne*, but after reading it I sincerely hope that everyone will be able to go into a restaurant with confidence and send back to the kitchens a *Tournedos Rossini* on which the chef has attempted to pass off a tired piece of liver sausage as a slice of *foie gras* – which has been known to happen.

I

CAVIARE

CAVIARE should not be served at cocktail parties on little bits of burnt toast.

If you must give yourself the illusion that you are impressing everyone by serving caviare, then you must do so in the grand style by providing your guests with half a dozen tins of the stuff into which they can dip freely, even if they are a little bit sick afterwards.

The eating of caviare has been regarded so much as a status symbol since Hamlet said: 'The play, I remember, pleased not the millions; 'twas caviare to the general', that thousands who talk about it with veneration or blasé contempt have never actually tasted the real thing.

There is no reason why they shouldn't have. You don't need a lot to enjoy it; an ounce is too little, but two ounces too much, and if you really appreciate the better things of life, spending a pound for a few mouthfuls of this delight now and then is not all that extravagant.

At any rate, before you damn it as a folly, try it – and do not just buy any old caviare, buy the best and the freshest and eat in a restaurant of repute, or at home in bed at twelve o'clock on a Sunday morning before you open your first bottle of champagne.

Though caviare immediately brings Russia to mind the word does not appear in the Russian language, where it is known as *ikra*. 'Caviare' is common to most European tongues and is derived from the Italian *caviala* or Turkish *khavyah*.

Its first mention in Europe was by Rabelais in his *Faits et dits héroiques du Grand Pantagruel* in 1533. Shakespeare obviously knew about it in England later in that century and in 1711 one reads on the subject of *khavia*, in Savary's *Dictionnaire du Commerce*, that it was not despised at the best of tables in France.

But what is this comestible that has irresistible appeal to the gourmet, doe-eyed models, dukes of the international set, kinky starlets and fat, innocent film producers? It is the prepared roe of a species of fish called *acipenser* which are caught in the Caspian and Black Seas.

There are three varieties of acipenser used in the production of caviare, the *Beluga*, the *Ocietrova* or sturgeon and the *Sevruga*. The name sturgeon is applied in everyday life to all these species, though, in fact, only the *Ocietrova* is a sturgeon.

Until the middle of the nineteenth century the rivers running into the Atlantic and Baltic were fairly rich in sturgeon, as were the Rhine and the North American lakes, but industry, steam navigation, dredging and poisonous factory discharges have caused their disappearance in these areas. Caviare now comes exclusively from Russia, Persia and Rumania.

The fish seek fresh water at spawning time, where they deposit their spawn on the bottom of the river for it to mature. Here the young fish find excellent conditions for growth after leaving the egg.

It is during the breeding season, when they leave the

deep sea waters and turn to the shallower river beds, that they are caught – but not killed. The roe at that time would be unsuitable for consumption, being so greasy as to be unpalatable.

As the Caspian and Black Seas experience very severe winters, ice-bound conditions make it impossible for the sturgeon to obtain sufficient food. Nature being what it is, however, they are capable of storing nourishment in their roes in times of plenty for the leaner months.

When the sturgeon are caught at spawning time they are therefore placed in submerged floating cages the size of large barges and, unable to search for food, use up their reserve. In due course they are killed, but only experienced hands can determine when the roes will be right for eating.

The trapping of sturgeons today is carried out efficiently with modern equipment and up-to-date methods, but before the revolution the swashbuckling Cossacks of the Ural Mountains were the caviare boys of their time, and they had elaborate ways of fishing.

They only went after the sturgeon for a fortnight, twice a year, and the whole population joined in on these occasions – the wives, the children, the grandparents, uncles, aunts and cousins – all with their tents, household goods, cooking utensils and other equipment piled on to their sleighs.

The first fortnight (*Plawnaja*) was in the autumn, when short drift nets were used and many hundreds of Cossacks participated, pulling the nets down the river and entangling the fish as they went.

The winter catch (*Bagornaja*) was made under the ice. A stretch of river was surrounded by a large number of the

Cossacks, armed with harpoons, and on the firing of a cannon, everyone made a hole in the ice and then endeavoured to harpoon the sturgeon which, frightened by the noise, flurried by beneath them.

When one spot had been fished to a finish, the cannons being fired at odd intervals to give a sense of drama to the occasion and also to frighten the poor fish to death, the Cossacks moved on downstream where the manoeuvre was repeated till the mouth of the river was reached.

Apart from the Cossacks and their families the river banks were crowded with rich dealers from Moscow, Leningrad and other parts of Europe, who followed the fishermen down the river in their carriages, bringing everything for the preparation of caviare with them. The freshly caught fish were sold to the highest bidder, eviscerated on the spot and the caviare, fresh or frozen, taken to the nearest railway station and dispatched.

Of the three varieties of acipenser mentioned, the *Beluga* is the largest, sometimes reaching a length of twelve feet and weighing up to 25 cwt – 130 lb. of caviare has been obtained from a single *Beluga*, the only cannibal in the tribe.

The *Ocietrova* (sturgeon) is next, growing to a length of six feet and weighing up to 400 lb. From a good specimen 40 lb. of roe can be obtained.

The *Sevruga* is much smaller and rarely exceeds four feet in length, weighing 60 lb. and only producing 8 lb. of caviare.

The roe is extracted and carefully sieved several times through fine mesh to remove the tissues and membranes from the eggs, which are then steeped in a brine solution.

The strength of the solution is very carefully controlled as the extent of salting determines an important quality of the caviare.

The best quality caviare is always slightly salted and is known as *malossol*. This word does not denote a separate caviare, but is a quality of grading applied to the roes. The salt content is three to four per cent.

The best malossol caviare is prepared from the spring fishing of sturgeon caught in the March to mid-April season, when the water is cool and the fish are firm and fresh. The autumn fishing does not produce such a fine quality caviare, the weather being much hotter and causing the roe to lose its firmness.

Caviare, prepared by the Russians in the malossol manner, is packed into 4-lb. tins, surrounded by ice in barrels and sent by refrigerated transport overland to Leningrad and then by sea to Europe and America. Throughout the whole process of packing and dispatch, government inspectors maintain a rigid control. The preparation of caviare in Persia and Rumania is similar, though probably less controlled by inspectors. Delivery is usually by air and is non-refrigerated.

Malossol caviare is not only a great delicacy but is very easily digested and an excellent pick-me-up for invalids. It is also highly nutritious, containing about 30 per cent protein and 16 per cent fat.

Another kind of caviare prepared in these areas is *pressed caviare*. After cleaning the eggs in the usual way the caviare is poured into linen bags and allowed to hang and drain much like cream cheese. This tends to destroy the natural shape of the small eggs as they are pressed together. The caviare is then packed in barrels holding about 100 lb. It has a much saltier taste than malossol, but is of the characteristic sturgeon flavour. There is, of course, no appearance of grain and it is usually a solid mass. Connoisseurs greatly prize it and the price is moderate in comparison with some of the other grades.

The various kinds of caviare have distinctive tastes and it by no means follows that the most expensive caviare necessarily has the best flavour.

Strange as it may seem, the market value of caviare is judged by its appearance, the larger grains being the more popular. The *Beluga* grain is the largest and varies in colour from dark steel grey to bluish white.

Ocietrova grains are a little smaller and usually preferred by regular caviare eaters. It is sometimes golden brown in colour, sometimes bottle green or, like *Beluga*, steel grey.

Sevruga, the smallest in size, is usually more stable in colour, dark green, sometimes black.

There are on the market other products which are sold under the label of caviare. Red caviare *(Keta)* is made from the salmon roe, a perfectly good product, bright orange in colour, but tasting more of cod's roe than anything else. Then there are other roes which, to the man in the street, look like caviare but, in fact, are not.

A number of European countries market these roes in jars and packs similar to caviare and go as far as calling the product caviare *style* or caviare *type*. My personal objections to these products are that, probably quite innocently, they mislead the general public into thinking that it is getting caviare cheap. It is not getting caviare and it is not even getting a substitute cheaply.

The real stuff can safely be recognized only by its price and by the fact that it will be labelled either *Beluga*, *Ocietrova* or *Sevruga*.

When caviare arrives in this country it is subjected to a duty of 30 per cent of the landed value, but it is offered in a wide price range to suit most people's pockets.

The original pack is broken down on arrival in Britain into smaller containers to suit the different types of trade. Fresh caviare is repacked in small tins and dispatched to restaurants, and, for the delicatessen and grocery shops, caviare is packed in glass jars and sometimes pasteurized.

Pasteurized caviare has a longer shelf life than fresh and need not necessarily be kept in a refrigerator. But all caviare keeps best in a temperature of exactly 32 degrees F. It is *fatal* to put caviare in a deep freeze, which will only result in one being left with a somewhat expensive soup.

Caviare importers, a noble band of five in this country, go to a great deal of trouble to store it at exactly the right temperature. From long experience it has been found that even a slight variation over a long period can spoil the quality.

Unopened jars and glasses can be kept quite satisfactorily a week or so in a domestic refrigerator but, once open, the contents of the pack should be eaten within a few days.

Exposure to air causes rapid deterioration, and any container should be covered and replaced immediately in the refrigerator.

Caviare is a delicate seafood, so delicate that it should be eaten solely as a unique experience and not drowned with wine or pints of vodka as is customary in all good Hollywood versions of life under the Tsars.

There is no ritual about eating caviare, the best way is to place a little on lightly (unsalted) buttered rye bread, pop it in the mouth and munch away. If rye bread is not available, toast is as good, or bliny, little pancakes made from a fermented batter of buckwheat. Caviare is sometimes rolled in bliny and served with sour cream. To really satisfy experienced palates, an ounce of caviare rolled in smoked salmon will produce mumbles of ecstasy.

Caviare in a restaurant can cost anything from 25s. to 60s. a portion. It is sometimes wiser to ask how much of a portion you are going to get. In most cases 1 oz. is considered to be suitable. I personally think this a little mean.

In a high-class grocery store the average price of caviare is 20s. an ounce. *Beluga* is always more expensive than *Ocietrova*. *Sevruga* is always the cheapest and can be obtained for around 15s. Over the counter it is sold in glass or earthenware jars which are usually returnable (they cost about 12s. themselves). Pressed caviare is sold in tubes, like toothpaste, but without free gift offers.

2

FOIE GRAS

STRASBOURG in Alsace, north-east France, on the Rhine, has a cathedral, a statue to Gutenberg (who did not invent printing), storks that bring babies at dawn to young married couples and *foie gras* by the ton.

An American, who was passing through this historic city, stopped for lunch at a sixteenth-century auberge one day and, not knowing what *foie gras* was, sought enlightenment. The patron, who was the chef, head waiter, cellarman and washer-up, rubbed his hands with glee, allowed his chest to swell with pride and spoke out:

'Rare, smooth, with a melting quality possessing a strong yet delicate aroma, whose lingering taste is fully savoured by the palate, *foie gras*, food of the gods, brings that touch of heavenly perfection and that unparalleled enjoyment of a delicacy to the French culinary art, without which it would remain incomplete!'

'Yes,' said the American politely. 'But what is it?'

'It is an experiment in ambrosia, Monsieur, it makes all conversation cease since the heart is overflowing with delight.'

'It certainly makes all conversation cease,' said the American less patiently. 'But just what is it? I mean, can I eat it with tomato sauce?'

The patron's answer is not recorded. Perhaps he died on the spot.

Foie gras, if literally translated, means fat liver, an unappetizing enough name for so talked about a dish. But the liver is no ordinary liver, nor is it just fat.

Foie gras is the resulting product of an extremely complicated process involving the liver of the goose, and its recipe dates back to 1762.

A lot has been written about the cruelty meted out to geese in order to obtain these livers. Folklore, traditional stories and old prints tell of farmers squeezing geese between their knobbly knees and ramming vast quantities of maize down their throats till they die of hypertrophied stomachs, but then old stories also tell of men hanging other men in public squares.

Today, as in everything, the special livers are obtained by more scientific methods. The goose is placed in a pen by itself and given plenty to eat: beetroot, Jerusalem artichokes, carrots, cooked potatoes, maize, oats and beans, with fresh water running continually in a gully through the pen. The mixture it is given contains a high percentage of vitamins and the goose, being a greedy creature, eats as much as it can hold. After two or three weeks of further treatment, the goose's liver swells slowly and when the breeder thinks it is ready, the bird is killed and the liver removed.

For the squeamish, who might raise a cry of protest at the killing of the goose, I would point out that nothing can be eaten without being killed – even a cabbage has a pretty rough time when being boiled. One forgets, for some reason, when chewing through a steak that some poor cow has perished by the electric mallet yet, when served with a pleasant little pheasant, one tends to dwell on the suffering the poor bird might have been through before being cooked. It's a mad world and I dare say that one day someone will eat us.

Once the goose livers have been selected by the breeder they are sent to the manufacturer of *foie gras* and, in some rare cases, to a chef who will make his own *pâté*. Generally, however, *foie gras* is bought direct from Strasbourg, either fresh or in tins, from specialists who have kitchens behind their shop premises, like *pâtissiers* and *charcutiers*.

The manufacturing of *foie gras* calls for very special care. When the bile has been removed from the livers, they must be carefully graded and sorted. This is a delicate operation which requires the intuition of the manufacturer and many years' experience. Some livers may be ideal for steaming, others for baking. Those which are suitable for light steaming would quickly become dry if cooked in an oven. The colour, texture and firmness are also important.

By skilful surgery, the nerves are removed from the livers, which are then put to soak in water for varying lengths of time and are then seasoned. After these preparations the actual manufacture takes place. The livers are stuffed with truffles, then steamed or cooked in the oven if they are to be eaten at once, or else put into earthenware jars or tins if they are to be preserved.

The procedure is always the same, but the length of cooking time varies. The livers of lesser quality or wrong colour (they should be shell pink) are pulverized into 'mousse' for sandwich spreads.

Foie gras is presented in various shapes and sizes and in different types of container. For restaurants it is packed in tins, for home consumption in earthenware terrines.

TYPES OF PÂTÉ DE FOIE GRAS AVAILABLE

Bloc tunnel de foie gras truffé – a tunnel-shaped length of *foie gras* specially prepared for slicing.

Terrines de foie gras truffé – *Foie gras* packed in decorated terrines suitable for one to twelve persons.

Pâtés de foie gras truffé en croûte – *Foie gras* pie. This long or cylindrical pie is filled with *foie gras*, coated with jelly, covered with edible crust. It is from this presentation that the name *pâté de foie gras* originates. Unfortunately many restaurants in England tend to sell *pâté de foie gras* when it is nothing of the sort – usually an ordinary liver pâté. Price is the one way of telling the genuine article, *foie gras* cannot be sold for less than 10s. a portion.

Suprême de foie gras truffé – a block of *foie gras* in aspic jelly. The jelly is usually flavoured with madeira.

Foie gras au naturel – unseasoned, not truffled, used in cooking for specialized dishes.

The delicate nature of *foie gras* necessitates particular care in serving. It is absolutely essential that it should be served cold and eaten at the beginning of a meal, so that the palate, as yet uncontaminated, is able to savour it to the full, and with a white wine – a Riesling, Champagne, White Burgundy or even, according to taste, a Bordeaux of good vintage. Red wines should definitely NOT be served as they detract from the taste instead of sharpening it.

Foie gras can be garnished with jelly but nothing else.

Nowadays the crime of serving it with salad is rarely committed, its delicate smoothness should never be mingled with the acidity of vinegar.

Foie gras is best presented on the plate in the shape of shells, scooped out of the terrine with a spoon – or in slices. The spoon or knife should first be dipped in hot water, the heated blades making the cutting easier.

Certain types of *foie gras* are surrounded by a thin layer of white fat. The connoisseur will remove this, knowing that it has only been used to ensure perfection in its preparation.

Foie gras has persisted throughout the ages, irrespective of changing events and the innovations of man. The reason for this is simple. From the moment of its creation, *foie gras* was at once considered to be a dish 'fit for a king', and to maintain its high standard, scrupulous traditional attention to the recipe has always been maintained.

As is the case with so many dishes of outstanding repute, *foie gras* owes its origin to a famous man.

Goose liver itself has been consumed for many centuries. Pliny speaks of 'the exquisite taste of the fattened goose liver'. Horace, before him, mentioned it in his Satires, Martial (A.D. 43) in his Epigrams and Juvenal (A.D. 130) also. Rabelais wrote about it, of course, along with Montaigne and other authors of the sixteenth century, but it was due to the Maréchal de Contades that it takes its place in history, having received official recognition at the Court of Versailles.

From 1762 to 1788 the Maréchal de Contades was Military Governor of the province of Alsace, and resided in

Strasbourg. His head chef was one Jean Pierre Clause, a native of neighbouring Lorraine, whose ability in the culinary arts was gratefully acknowledged by the guests of the Maréchal.

One day, in an effort to give pleasure to his master, he put before him his *Pâté à la Contades*, a dish which he had just invented.

The Maréchal thought it so magnificent that he had a second 'pâté' made immediately and sent straight away by messenger to Versailles.

The King and his Court were so delighted with this new exquisite dish that the Maréchal was granted an estate in Picardy, while the chef, who after all invented the recipe, received a present of twenty pistoles.

The *foie gras* of Strasbourg had won the coveted approval of the Court, which was considered to be the supreme authority on matters of good taste, and that set the seal on its march towards the world-wide fame it enjoys today.

Not long after, Clause left the service of the Maréchal and in 1784 married the widow of a pastrycook. He set up business with her in her first husband's shop and began to make *pâté de foie gras* (which until then had been made exclusively for the Maréchal) for the citizens of Strasbourg.

From this source has been handed down the trade secret, so carefully guarded, which still maintains the universal reputation of the *foie gras de Strasbourg*.

Foie gras in tins and terrines is available at all good high-class grocers.

There are a number of brands, the most famous of which

is F. FEYEL, whose premises lie in the shadows of Strasbourg cathedral.

Prices vary, but a two-portion terrine is unlikely to cost less than 25s. Tins cost less, but again a good portion will work out at about 10s. When purchasing terrines and tins it is best to examine the stated content – not all terrines contain the same weight of *foie gras*, though they may have similar size-numbers.

Foie gras is also produced in the Périgord and the Landes, but the quality cannot be compared to that of Alsace.

3

OYSTERS

LADY SMART: Will you eat any oysters before dinner?
COLONEL ATWIT: With all my heart. He was a bold man that
first ate an oyster.
LADY SMART: They say oysters are a cruel meat, because we
eat them alive; then they are an uncharitable meat, for we
leave nothing to the poor; and they are an ungodly meat,
because we never say grace.

Polite Conversation, Jonathan Swift, 1731.

John Gay, some years earlier, was also inspired to write
about the first man to eat oysters.

> The man had sure a palate covered o'er
> With brass or steel, that on the rocky shore
> First broke the oozy oyster's pearly coat
> And risked the living morsel down his throat.

However brave or admired this man was, all that can be
presumed about him is that he lived before a certain
Roman, Sergius Aurata, who founded an oyster farm in
Southern Italy in 102 B.C. – the first record in history of
oysters being bedded for consumption in quantity.

The Greeks loved oysters and used their shells for casting votes, scratching their choice of politician on the white
mother of pearl with a sharp instrument. The Celts fed on
oysters, but neither the Egyptians nor Assyrians have ever

claimed to, and there is no mention of the delicious bivalve mollusc in the Bible.

We know that Cicero (106–43 B.C.) nourished his eloquence with the dainty, that Louis XI fêted the learned professors of the Sorbonne once a year on oysters 'lest their scholarship should become deficient' and that one of Napoleon's marshals regularly consumed a hundred as a light prelude to his breakfast proper – which may be the reason why the French have the largest oyster farm in the world.

This farm, at Arcachon, on the Bay of Biscay, came into being by accident. A large consignment of elongated Portuguese oysters were the unfortunate passengers aboard a cargo boat that sank in a storm at the mouth of the Gironde. These shipwrecked oysters, however, survived the adventure without too much trouble and, liking the surroundings, settled down to a healthy bit of breeding and became, in time, the founder members of the vast colony.

Extremely grateful for this extraordinary piece of luck, the French took it for granted that they were now the possessors of an inexhaustible supply. However, they soon came to realize that unless the mollusc was protected, the enormous national consumption would soon cause a shortage.

In 1750 the gathering of oysters in the Bay of Arcachon was therefore forbidden for four years, to give the creatures time to reproduce in peace, and after that it became illegal to collect them between May and October. This law, together with a well-publicized rumour that oysters in the breeding season could be injurious to health, started the tradition that they should never be eaten in an R-less month, though most oysters can, in fact, be eaten all year round.

There are two types of oyster, the wild and the cultivated. The former settles on the rocky sea-bed unattended at a depth of anything between eighteen to a hundred and eighty feet, the latter is carefully nursed by man through all its phases of growth – not so much for love as for money.

The cultivated kind are reared in farms some way out at sea till they grow to a certain size. They are then transferred to beds near the mouth of a river. Here the mixture of sea and fresh water induces a faster fattening process, but they do not live for long in water containing less than three per cent of salt.

British cultured oysters take about four years to grow to a diameter of two and a half inches, but in South Carolina an American variety has reached the same size in eight months.

The most popular varieties in Europe are the Belon, Blue Point, Colchester, Cornish, Loch Ryan, Marenne Verte, Ostend, Portuguese, Whitstable and Zeeland. Of these the *Portuguese* is an outsider, having an irregular curved shell, one valve of which is smaller than the other.

The provision of suitable perches for the oyster is essential, and artificial beds consist of a network of stakes on which the seed oyster is affixed. Often the beds are raised by means of wires so that the shells are exposed to the rain for a while, fresh water killing off one of the oyster's worst enemies – the boring sponge.

Even when the greatest care is taken, oysters are still

and butter, there are a number of more elaborate recipes. Whichever way you choose to eat your oyster, however, you cannot escape the fact that it has to be opened.

Some people attack them with a hammer, which can lead to great hardship for both parties. An eccentric once used a pneumatic drill in desperation. In America the problem has been overcome by a machine which drives a wedge-shaped piece of metal between the two halves of the shell, but the old-fashioned, traditional method is still probably the quickest and the best.

If you purchase oysters to consume at home, you should arm yourself with a large cloth and an oyster knife, which has a stiff blade $3\frac{1}{2}$ inches long and a half-inch wide, tapering slightly to a rounded (not pointed) end, with a good handle.

Gripping the oyster firmly in the cloth you should attempt to prise open the shells by inserting the blade alongside the hinge, the point where the growth-rings start radiating. After a struggle you will eventually exhaust the oyster by twisting the knife backwards and forwards at the said point. When you get in, you should cut through the muscle hinging the two shells and discard the one you are not going to use.

Some people prefer eating the oyster off the flat shell, but most prefer to have it served in the deeper shell, which holds all the liquor. The oyster should first be scooped out and turned over so that it can easily be forked out or slipped straight from the shell into the mouth.

Oysters vary greatly in price, depending on the season, and the time in the season. Some restaurants add 100 per cent, some hardly anything. It is unlikely that you will get them cheaper than 6s. a dozen, though in some sea-coast towns they sell occasionally at fourpence each.

The size of the oyster naturally determines the price; what should be borne in mind by the consumer is its freshness. Fish restaurants that sell oysters regularly and have a daily delivery are obviously the best.

Oysters should be eaten accompanied by a dry white wine. A Meursault, Petit Chablis, a Graves *frappé* (iced), a Sylvaner or a Champagne.

If you enjoy oysters and wish to change occasionally from eating them raw you can indulge in fried, grilled or devilled oysters, oyster soup or Angels on Horseback.

The latter is an appetizer of grilled oysters wrapped in bacon, sprinkled with breadcrumbs and served on toast.

Fried oysters are poached beforehand, dipped in milk and flour, deep fried then served with lemon and fried parsley.

Grilled oysters, also called devilled oysters, are poached, threaded on to a metal skewer, seasoned with salt, pepper and lemon, dipped in melted butter and breadcrumbs, then grilled.

Oyster soup is usually made up of boiled oysters in white wine with cream, crushed biscuit crackers, butter and Cayenne pepper.

Oysters are also served *à l'Américaine, à la Nantua, à la Florentine, à la Mornay, au gratin,* etc ... a résumé can be found in the glossary.

For those who may be disappointed by the fact that they are unlikely to find a pearl among their oysters and so become rich during the course of a dinner, there is still some hope. One oyster is known to have brought fame and fortune to its owner.

A hundred years ago the proprietor of a restaurant in Drury Lane was disturbed in the night by the sound of a whistle repeated at regular intervals. Believing himself to be the victim of a gang of housebreakers he crept downstairs armed with a stick.

Stealthily he made his way to the kitchens, where the whistling came from, and soon realized that one of the intruders was in the larder. Flinging the door open he got ready to club the criminal but found the place empty. The deafening whistle persisted however.

After listening to this strange sound for some minutes he traced it to a large oyster barrel in the corner and, to his amazement, eventually fished out the culprit.

One oyster had a small hole pierced in its upper shell. When it breathed, water was forced through this aperture, causing the whistle.

The next night the oyster set fashionable London alight, and its owner was host to Thackeray and Dickens, among a stream of other celebrities who came to listen to the musical mollusc while gobbling up dozens of its less talented cousins.

4

SMOKED SALMON

ANYBODY can smoke salmon, providing they can get the right type of salmon to smoke. It is the fish itself that is expensive, not the process to which it is subjected, though the expert skill of the pickler, the splitter and smoker are not negligible.

Few people south of the border bother to smoke their own salmon, but in Scotland there are still people who fish it and smoke it at the bottom of their gardens, hoteliers in particular finding it more profitable.

The smoking of salmon is simple – in theory. Before smoking any fish it must be pickled in a brine, that is water with enough salt in it to float a potato. In the case of salmon this takes up to three or four days.

Once out of the brine the salmon should be scaled, a dozen or so diamond-shaped pieces of skin removed on both sides where the skin is thickest and a pinch of salt-petre rubbed into the exposed flesh. The salmon should then be filleted, all bones being removed except the stiff collar bones under the gill covers, which can serve as supports to hang the fish by when in the smoke box.

The salmon should then be placed in a tray and covered with a thin layer of moist brown sugar and coated with a similar quantity of coarse salt, left for twenty-four hours and turned over to repeat the process. After that it should be washed and swabbed and hung in the smoke box.

The making of the box is child's play. All you need do is dig a trench a foot wide, a foot deep and ten feet long, in the direction of a prevailing wind, at one end of which you place an inverted packing-case which has been carefully papered over so that all the cracks have been sealed. You will also have carefully arranged a hinged lid, a tubular vent in the centre and metal bars running across it inside.

At the other end of the ten-foot trench you light a fire and, between the fire and the box, unload a barrowful of oak sawdust. When the fire is glowing a bright red, you cover the trench with paving stones, iron sheets or other non-flammable material, and spread earth over these, sealing the trench like a tunnel.

Once the sawdust has started smouldering, the smoke should flow along the tunnel and out of the little tubular vent, having passed through and filled the packing-case. It is then that you whip open the lid and hang your salmon from the metal bars, after which you close the lid and leave the whole ingenious piece of equipment for forty-eight hours.

When you return you will open the lid and either find that your fire has gone out, the salmon has been burnt to a cinder because you left too much draught somewhere, or that you have a beautifully smoked salmon.

A simpler method of getting smoked salmon is, of course, to order it in a restaurant. The thin, delicate pink slices of fish set before you will have been through a very similar process.

On a commercial basis the smoking of salmon is naturally more scientifically carried out. The best salmon are bought from Scotland, but some come from Ireland and Scandinavia.

Whole salmon selected for smoking never weigh less than 12 lb., the best weighing from 15 lb. to 25 lb. Each is thoroughly washed and split by hand, lengthwise, with the expert incision of a huge machete-like knife.

Once the fish has been split the bones are taken out, leaving the two filleted halves. These are placed in trays, sugared and salted and left for certain periods of time. They are then again washed and hooked up in an air-controlled drying room for twenty-four hours. The air in these drying rooms circulates continually and is maintained at a temperature of 80 degrees F.

When dry the salmon sides are hung in great black funnels through which smoke from smouldering oak sawdust passes. The sides are smoked for twelve or twenty-four hours, depending on the size and quality of the fish.

Because a salmon is smoked it does not mean that it is preserved. A salmon, correctly smoked, with only a minimum of salt added for preservation, will keep its freshness as long as a bottle of milk. Smoked salmon, in fact, should be treated like milk and put back in the refrigerator when not immediately required.

Approximately two million pounds of smoked salmon are consumed in the British Isles every year. With this huge demand it is not surprising that the necessary number of fish are hard to come by and the supplies in the Scottish and Irish rivers steadily decreasing. There was a time when English rivers, including the Thames, provided large catches of salmon, but the last recorded catch was in 1908.

It is known that the smoking of salmon was practised in

Russia in the middle of the eighteenth century, a practice which was keenly appreciated by Jewish families, who probably made the delicacy popular throughout the western world. One of the first commercial enterprises was founded in London in 1879 and 90 per cent of the trade was then for the Jewish community. Gradually, however, smoked salmon began to be widely appreciated and now it is the most popular of all luxury foods, not only served as an hors d'œuvre, but used in sandwiches in great abundance and recommended by doctors to patients who have inhospitable stomachs.

Salmon are anadromous, that is they migrate from the sea to fresh-water rivers to spawn. Some species go right upstream to the river source, while others spawn in the lower stretches. Some salmon, in Canada, have been found over a thousand miles from the sea.

Salmon usually leave the sea in good condition, but on entering fresh water they stop feeding and sometimes wear themselves out trying to reach distant places to deposit their eggs. They will jump rapids and falls, often leaping right out of the water to heights several times their own length. For some inexplicable reason they set out with the inborn determination to spawn in the same spot where they themselves were hatched and find their birthplace by instinct.

The female makes a trough in the river bed where she deposits her eggs, then the male drifts over these and fertilizes them. The female covers the eggs with any material she can find on the river bed and both she and her partner then let themselves be swept down the river. By the time they have spawned both are often in a dilapidated condition, but whether in good or bad health, they invariably die after spawning, seemingly losing complete interest in life. Salmon never spawn more than once.

The eggs hatch within seventy days. The newly hatched fish, weak and helpless at first, remain hidden for a long period among the pebbles, then start searching for food. They remain in this environment for anything up to a year then descend the rivers to the sea. The fish matures when it is between two and seven years old and, sometimes during that period, gets the urge to spawn which causes it to re-enter fresh water and start the hard fight back to the hatching ground to begin the whole exhausting cycle again.

Salmon are cannibals, and their nourishment consists of post larvae of herrings and other fish. They can live without going to sea at all, and certain species do so in Norway and Sweden, where they inhabit fresh-water lakes, leaving the lakes for the rivers at spawning time and returning to the lakes as others return to the sea. This also happens in the Canadian lakes, but generally such salmon do not develop very quickly.

Salmon vary greatly in size. On average they grow to a length of four feet, weighing 14 lb. In Scotland salmon have been caught weighing up to 70 lb.

The flesh of the salmon, which is pale peach in colour, becomes bright pink when cooked. It is extremely delicate, though fatty and, to some, indigestible.

Apart from being smoked, salmon is eaten cooked, whole, or served in chunks or cutlets. Poached in a flavoured *court-bouillon* it is served cold with a mayonnaise, a *sauce tartare*, a *sauce verte*, a *rémoulade* or *sauce vincent*, and hot with anchovy, butter, shrimp, caper, lobster, *mousseline*, *nantua*, *ravigote* or *venetienne* sauce. There are many recipes for serving salmon, all well worth trying.

Smoked salmon can be purchased at any good fishmonger's and is served in most restaurants. If you wish to give it to guests at home you can either buy a side – which will weigh between 3 lb. and 4 lb. – or buy it by the pound already sliced. If you are not an expert the latter is advisable. If you are adventurous, the side should be placed on a wooden board larger than the side itself, tacked to it discreetly with a nail at the tail end and sliced with an extremely sharp knife all along the surface, always cutting towards the head end.

The sliced sliver, which should be as long as possible and the width of the salmon, should be placed covering the plate and set before the glutton with a slice of lemon, a pepper mill within reach and brown bread and butter.

In a restaurant a four-ounce portion, which is considered generous, may cost anything from 10s. to 17s. 6d. depending on the time of year and the restaurant's reputation. It is unlikely that you will get served anything but Scotch salmon in a good place.

Scotch salmon is far more expensive than Baltic salmon, which is the usual alternative at any fishmongers. A side of Scotch will cost about 35 per cent more than Baltic salmon. The taste and quality of the flesh explain the difference. Scotch salmon is far superior and Baltic salmon is, in fact, mainly used for sandwiches or served in small portions as part of an hors d'œuvres.

With developments in frozen foods and advances in the

preservation of highly-perishable articles there are few products which cannot be served at any time of the year, but the season for catching salmon runs from 11 February to the end of August. During that time the fish will be at its prime and the prices most reasonable.

Salmon, like any other fish, should be accompanied by a white wine – a Chablis, Montrachet, Pouilly, Loupiac, Meursault, Silvaner, Crépy, Muscadet, Traminer, Monbazillac, Vouvray, etc.

5

LOBSTERS AND CO.

And like a lobster boiled, the morn
From black to red began to turn.
SAMUEL BUTLER, 1612–1680.

. . . Which tells us that either mornings were painful to Mr Butler or that he thought a lobster's death was beautiful.

Whichever it was, the lobster is still boiled today, if lucky, if not, it suffers the indignity of being quartered, or halved to be precise – by the thick blunt knife of the *chef poissonier* (the point of the knife being inserted at the junction of the tail shells and body, where the spinal cord is situated, and the blade brought crushingly down like a guillotine, splitting the animal in half).

The sad fact about lobsters, crawfish, crayfish, prawns, shrimps, crabs and the like, is that they are impossible to kill without boiling or dismembering.

Though, no doubt, the majority of cooks would like to do something about the crustacea's predicament, they cannot allow themselves to become sentimental over the animals, and have to be cruel to earn their keep. But an attempt was made on the shellfish's behalf by an American marine biologist from New Jersey, to save them some pain during their last hour.

This noble scientist made a great number of experiments

to find out which was the least agonizing way of being boiled – whether the lobsters preferred the direct immersion method or the slow-heat process.

When plunged alive into the boiling water it was found that the animals definitely objected, making violent attempts to get out, and even squeaking. Death, it was calculated, was not anything like instantaneous, and the lobsters lived in great discomfort for at least fifty-eight seconds before giving up the ghost.

On the other hand when these noble shellfish were placed in cold water and brought slowly to the boil, they were quite passive, showing no signs of rebelliousness, nor making any attempt to escape. When the water reached a temperature of 70 degrees C. they gradually swooned and fell on their sides and at 80 degrees C. could safely be pronounced dead.

For those who would rather cook the lobsters themselves at home than have a namby-pamby chef serving it up with tears in his eyes, a word of warning.

You should always buy lobsters alive. If they are sold to you dead you cannot tell how long they have been in that condition nor what they have died of. If they are red, and therefore boiled, you still cannot tell how long they have been in that state and lobsters, specially in warm weather, have the tendency to deteriorate rapidly. So always order your lobsters well in advance and send them back to the fishmonger if they are not delivered to your door alive and pinching.

Lobsters are usually packed in large fish-boxes and comfortably bedded in dark seaweed so that animal and vegetable are difficult to tell apart. Study the mass carefully before lifting one of the creatures out for, if one lobster has managed to undo the string round its claws, it might take a sudden liking to your finger and this could prove fatal to your career as a violinist.

To lift a lobster from a mass of seaweed you should pick it up at the head shell by thumb and forefinger, where the claws cannot reach you – but a steady eye should be kept on the tail, which sometimes has the habit of flaying out at any human being in its way.

Lobsters have smooth shells and are a rich dark blue in colour, tinged with purple. Their joints are orange and their feelers bright red. Colourful animals when alive, they are even gayer when dead, turning bright crimson, their livers changing from messy brown to pastoral green.

They have five pairs of legs, the front pair having six segments each and terminating in huge pincers, one of which is larger and more powerful than the other. This is the dangerous crushing claw. The two pairs of legs behind it also have pincers, but much smaller, and the remaining two just have hoof-like ends.

Lobsters reach full growth very slowly. At five years of age they are just over four inches long, but attain a length of twelve to fourteen inches within eight years – weighing anything up to ten pounds.

While growing, the lobster sheds its tail, and does so some twenty times during its life. Female lobsters carry their eggs under the tail, and it is when the eggs are formed, but not laid, that the flesh is at its most delicious.

Lobsters live in shallow rocky water and are trapped with wickerwork pots or creels, or hoops covered with netting. These have funnel-shaped entrances allowing the lobster to get in but not out. The pots are baited with pieces of stale fish and sunk where the crustacea are known to be. Some two million are caught in European waters every year.

Lobsters are found along most European coasts from Norway to the Mediterranean. The American lobster, a variety rather than a different species, is found mostly along the east coast of the United States. It differs from its European cousin in size and colour, reaching a length of ten inches in five years and being dark bottle green. The largest lobster ever caught was two feet long with a twenty-inch girth and armed with pincers fifteen inches long, powerful enough to snip off a man's arm.

Those who enjoy titillating their palates with cooked crustacea will be able to tell the subtle difference between the lobster and the crawfish. The French much prefer the crawfish, but admit that the lobster has the advantage of having the claw meat which is exceptionally delicate.

The crawfish is sometimes called 'spiny lobster', but this is erroneous as the lobster has claws while the crawfish hasn't. There is also often some confusion between the crawfish and the crayfish, which is a fresh-water lobster, and in turn between the crayfish and the French *crevette*, which is a shrimp, which, in turn, is confused with the *crevette rose*, which is a prawn. To make it all clear, here is a simple Who's Who to shellfish society.

CRAB – French: *Crabe, Calappe, Poupart, Tourteau, Gourballe*. Four legs and one claw on each side of a flying-saucer-type shell body.

CRAWFISH – French: *Langouste*. No claws, smaller than the lobster, caught off the Devon and Cornish coasts in abundance.

CRAYFISH – French: *Écrevisse*. Fresh-water lobster. Two varieties, one large, one small. Usually about four inches long.

LOBSTER – French: *Homard*.

PRAWN – French: *Crevette Rose*. About two inches long. The black filament in the back of prawns is poisonous to people who are allergic to shellfish – it should be removed before eating.

DUBLIN BAY PRAWN – French: *Langoustine*. Italian: *Scampi*. The largest and best of all prawns.

SHRIMP – French: *Crevette*.

The lobster is the basis of one of the most famous dishes in the world, *Homard à l'Américaine*. This dish, however, is not only famous for its delicacy but because it is the subject of a hundred-year-old controversy among epicures.

The basis of *Homard à l'Américaine* is raw lobster sautéed in oil, served with a rich, thick tomato and white wine sauce, a characteristic Mediterranean preparation.

Though it is believed by most that the recipe comes from America (*à l'Américaine!*) many famous French gastronomes are convinced that the dish originated in Nice in 1860, when *Langouste de la Méditerranée* was first prepared with tomatoes and white wine.

The title *Homard à l'Américaine*, they believe, must have been given to the dish by a Provence chef who went to America, where he served the sauce with raw lobster, instead of with crawfish, knowing that the crawfish was not appreciated in the States. The dish then came back to France as *Homard à l'Américaine*.

To add to this controversy, however, a number of Northern French chefs claim that the recipe originates from Brittany or a part of Brittany known as Armorique, and that *Homard à l'Américaine* is just a mis-spelling of *Homard à l'Armoriquaine*.

With lobster, or any shellfish, a number of white wines can be recommended – Chablis, Montrachet, Pouilly, Riesling, Champagne, extra dry.

The price of lobsters varies with the season of the year. In most restaurants a cooked lobster, or one served cold with mayonnaise and usual decorations, will be around 17s. 6d. per portion.

From a fishmonger, alive, anything from 10s., depending on the size.

6

WILD BOAR AND OTHER BEASTIES

At Christmas time be careful of your fame;
See the old tenants table be the same.
Then if you would send up the brawner's head,
Sweet rosemary and bays around it spread;
His foaming tusks let some large pippin grace,
Or 'midst those thundering spears an orange place,
Sauce like himself, offensive to its foes,
The roguish mustard, dangerous to the nose,
Sack and the well-spiced Hippocras the wine,
Wassail the bowl, with ancient ribbands fine,
Porridge with plumbs, and turkeys with the chine.

WILLIAM KING, 1708

TODAY the serving of a genuine wild boar's head is rare, for the simple reason that genuine wild boars are rare, but in the past this ferocious, ugly beast and its head would be seen at every banquet, for it was as famous and as Royal as the lion.

The Romans were first in on the act of having the boar as the main attraction during a banquet. Petronius, who died in A.D. 65, described such an occasion:

... The slaves spread coverings on our couches which had hunters with their hunting spears embroidered; in fact, the whole hunting scene embroidered on them. We did not as yet know what this meant when, suddenly, a great noise was heard outside and Laconian hounds rushed into the room and began running around the table. They were followed by a platter on which lay the most enormous wild boar. On its head was perched a cap of a freed slave; on his tusks hung down two baskets lined with palm leaves, one was filled with Syrian dates, the other with Theban dates, little sucking pigs, made of pastry and baked in the oven surrounded the animal as if pressing on the teats, thus giving the guests enough indication to see that it was a breeding sow that was served them.

Drawing his hunting knife, a slave gave the wild boar a great stab in the belly and suddenly, from the opening in the animal's side flew out thrushes. Vainly the birds tried to escape, flying round and round the room, bird-catchers, provided with fowler's rods, instantly caught them and, by order of the master offered one to each guest.

Later Juvenal, possibly suffering from indigestion, recorded the thought in A.D. 140: 'Oh what gluttony is his who has whole boars served up for himself, an animal born for banquets.'

Due to the fact that the boar was always fast, strong, very bad tempered, and could invariably be relied upon to turn nasty when cornered, it was considered the favourite beast of the chase and, in countless paintings, tapestries, frescoes, it has been shown being hunted, chased by dogs, trapped in nets, speared, or brought on with pomp at banquets.

Richard III (1452–85) had the boar as his emblem, and Shakespeare, though not writing a sonnet about the animal, gives it a part in Henry V as an inn sign. Act II Scene

1 opens with Bardolph and Pistol meeting before the Boar's Head Tavern, Eastcheap.

The Boar's Head as a traditional dish travelled across the Atlantic in the *Mayflower*, with the Pilgrim Fathers. Jane G. Austin, the nineteenth-century American novelist, in her book *Betty Alden*, describes the following:

Plenty of trenchers both of pewter and wood lined the table, and by each lay a napkin and a spoon, but neither knives nor forks, the latter implements not having yet been invented, except in the shape of a powerful trident to lift the boiled beef from the kettle, while table knives, as Priscilla Alden had intimated, were still regarded as curious implements of extreme luxury. A knife of a different order, sometimes a clasp knife, sometimes a sheath knife, or even a dagger, was generally carried by each man, and used upon certain *pièces de résistance*, such as a boar's head, a roasted peacock, a shape of brawn, a powdered and cloved and browned ham, or other such triumphs of the culinary art as must be served whole. Such dishes were carried around the table, and every guest, taking hold of the morsel he coveted with his napkin, sliced it off with his own knife, displaying the elegance of his table manners by the skill with which he did it.

The wild boar has long been extinct in the British Isles, but it is still found in marshy woodland districts where there is plenty of cover, in parts of Austria, France, Germany, Russia, and Spain, where it is still hunted. It is believed to have been responsible for the original stock from which all races of domestic pigs have been raised.

The boar's head, presented at banquets today, or more often forming the centre-piece of a cold buffet table at Christmas, will be one of three types: the true wild boar's head, the disguised pig's head, or the modelled, glazed replica of the real boar's head.

Dressing a real wild boar's head is a long process, taking at least a fortnight in all. The head of the wild boar is severed from the rest of the body, as long in the neck as possible, and the ears are cut off to be dealt with separately.

The head is then soaked in water, cleaned, shaved completely, singed so that no hair is left and boned so that nothing but the outer skin remains. This is an expert's job worthy of a top embalmer's skill.

Once the mask of the head has been separated, a mixture of salt, saltpetre, brown sugar, ground pimentos, ground mace, powdered marjoram, and garlic is rubbed by hand into the skin, once every day for a fortnight.

During this time the meat from the rest of the boar is chopped up, seasoned, and cooked and mixed with diced tongue, salt pork, truffles, pistachio nuts, garlic, eggs and parsley and made into a rich brawn.

When the treated skin is ready, this brawn is stuffed into it, packed tightly so as to fill every fold, pushing out every original feature, and the whole is then wrapped in a damp cloth and tied up very tightly with string in the shape of the boar's head.

This bundle is then cooked for four hours in a jelly stock, allowed to cool, then unwrapped. The head, now looking like its old self, but without eyes, teeth or ears, is then dipped into a dark gelatine to regain some of its more natural colour, the shaved skin being pinkish and blotchy.

Once the dark gelatined head is dry, the decoration begins. First the original ears, nicely trimmed and cleaned and browned in dark jelly, are put back, then the eyes, made of whites of egg and truffles, a calf's tongue *à l'écarlate* is skewered into the mouth, and the tusks, thoroughly cleaned and bleached, replaced in their own position, but at the angriest angle. The top of the head and the surround is decorated with aspics and attelets (little utensils in the shape of skewers with ornamented tops on which truffles, fruit, cock's comb, crayfish or other decorative foods are threaded) and sometimes a lemon is stuck in the boar's mouth for good measure.

The head is usually laid on a silver platter, or better still a gold one, and either placed in the centre of the high table or brought in with much ado, a blare of trumpets and the waving of flags, by two exhausted chefs.

Dressed wild boar's head is a cold dish and is eaten nowadays as an hors d'œuvres, though its spicy brawn is suitable as a dish by itself. It is sliced from the back, straight down, working steadily towards the snout.

The real wild boar's head is virtually unobtainable now in this country without a great deal of planning. Someone, somewhere in the wilder parts of Europe must first find a boar, catch up with it, kill it and then ship it to this country. But a decorated pig's head is as common as a York ham and can be ordered at any high-class butcher's or grocer's, or in a restaurant, without any difficulty at all.

The recipe for the decorated pig's head is the same as for the wild boar's head, only the head is less troublesome to prepare and, of course, much smaller. The price will depend entirely on what goes into the brawn, and the chef's personal fee.

The modelled glazed replica of the real wild boar's head

is the exclusive product of a firm of manufacturers and importers of high-class table delicacies in London.

The recipe, that of a French master *charcutier*, was invented for a special client, more by accident than management.

During the shooting of the film 'The Private Life of Henry VIII', in which Charles Laughton played the name part, and was seen devouring whole pheasants, sucking pigs, barons of beef and the like, a dressed wild boar's head was also to be brought on for his consumption in one of the banqueting scenes.

Even in 1933 wild boars' heads were hard to come by, and the property department at the studios hunted around for some time before being recommended to this firm, who knew about boars' heads, having supplied the Court of Queen Victoria with many in the past. Without difficulty hunters were contacted in Austria, a boar was hunted and killed and the beast eventually shipped over to London, cooked and dressed in the firm's kitchens.

Film business being what it is, however, no one worried too much about the boar's head when it arrived at the studio, and for a day or two it hung around till eventually the poor thing perished and only made its presence known by casting unpleasant odours unbearably near Anne Boleyn's dressing-room.

Another was ordered immediately, but this time got no farther than a corner of the carpenters' workshop. Another melted under the arc lamps during a very long 'take', a fourth came to a sticky end when the plaster imitation gold platter gave way under its weight, and when a fifth was ordered the firm reluctantly had to announce that no more boars could be found by the hunters as it was the wrong season of the year.

Panic! The director was waiting to shoot the banqueting scene and the property department couldn't find another boar! It was going to be a painful business for someone.

In desperation the head of continuity begged the firm to help him out, somehow, and the chef sat down to think.

At the eleventh hour he came up with an idea. Using a block of highly spiced brawn, he modelled the shape of a wild boar's head with a stuffing paste, which he then dipped into a large gelatine and decorated as though it were the real thing. The effect was good, if not better, than the true boar. The property department were delighted and promptly ordered thirty – one head for every day of the month to come – they were taking no more chances.

The banqueting scenes were shot, and re-shot, the studio staff fed on boar's head for a month. It all cost someone a fortune and eventually, when the director and editor came to cut the film they decided that the banqueting scene wasn't too well lit – so it was cut out. But from this exciting venture the modelled glazed replica of the wild boar's head was born, and it can be purchased today, from the same firm or direct from high-class grocery stores, any time of the year for festive occasions.

The heads vary in size – miniature ones weighing 8 lb., huge ones weighing twenty or over. Average price – 10s. per lb.

VENISON

Though the name 'venison' used to apply to the flesh of any sort of game or wild beast it is now restricted to the flesh of the roe deer, fallow deer, red deer, moose deer and reindeer.

The meat of the buck is tastier than that of the doe, but it should be eaten when the animal is young, or not older than three.

Venison meat is dry and a little tough, and the quarter of venison has to be rubbed with a mixture of flour and pepper and hung for three or four days in a cool, dry place before being marinated for a fortnight to three weeks. The best parts are the haunch, fillet, loin and chops.

Venison is at its most delicious when roasted on a spit and served with boiled french beans and red currant jelly.

ALLIGATOR

A species of the American crocodile, called Cayman, has been found to be quite palatable and is served in certain Paris restaurants and has formed part of the menu at eccentric dinners in London.

The reptile's feet are the part to eat, though the flesh tastes a little musky. *Alligator à l'Indienne* is worth trying, but it is not commonly stocked at fishmongers, and therefore not on most menus. Tact is required when ordering it in a restaurant as the waiter may think you are making fun of him.

Alligator, as yet, has not been preserved in any form, the canning industry believing that it might fail as a commercial proposition.

BEAR

Bear meat must be marinated for a long time before it is eaten. It is tough, though bears' paws are considered a great delicacy in the East.

Mencius, the great Chinese philosopher after Confucius, said: 'Fish is what I like, so are bears' paws; but if I cannot have both I will forgo the fish and have the bear's paw.'

The paw is packed in clean mud and baked in an oven. When the mud has hardened like clay and been allowed to cool it is cracked and torn off the paw. The hairy skin comes with it.

The paw meat is then simmered in water for a very long time until all the gamey smell has gone. It is served with a rich sauce and sliced like ham.

Though its supply is very limited it is not unobtainable. Before the last war a club of eminent eccentrics organized an annual banquet to consume exotic foods. One year they decided to try bear and ordered a beast from the same firm that specialized in the boars' heads.

The bear was purchased in Canada and shipped over. On arrival at the docks, two directors of the firm went to see it through the Customs and arrived just as the casket containing the bear was being lowered by crane from the ship's hold to the dockside.

The directors, aware that the bear had caught the imagination of certain newspapermen, were astonished to find that it was being given extraordinary VIP treatment by the authorities. Not only had the foreman asked his men to stand in a line, but, as the bear was lowered, everyone removed their hats and bowed.

Not until the box had been uncoupled and the label 'SKINNED BEAR – FOR HUMAN CONSUMPTION' read out, was the mystery revealed. The dockers had been told that the casket contained a deceased person.

CAMEL

Aristophanes said that it was served to Royalty, and he loved it. The hump, the stomach and the feet are those parts eaten by connoisseurs, and among the recipes recommended are: camel *cous-cous*, roast camel's fillet, camel's paunch *à la Marocaine*, camel pilaf, and *Ragoût de Chameau à la Tomate*. The camel has one hump, the dromedary two.

HAGGIS

Though not a beast, this is as good a place as any to put this strange, if not exactly luxurious, food. What is luxurious about haggis is its presentation. Haggis should never be brought into a room without being accompanied by an escort of bagpipes.

A haggis is made with the stomach of a sheep which is cleaned thoroughly and turned inside out. Spread over it is a mince of boiled heart, liver and lungs, spiced with salt, pepper, nutmeg, cayenne pepper and chopped onion. To this mince is added grated liver, oatmeal and chopped beef suet.

The stomach is wrapped round the mince and sewn up like a bag, but before the final slit is closed a glassful of rich gravy is poured in. The whole is then boiled for three hours in plenty of water.

Haggis is served with whisky – Scotch whisky.

OTHER EDIBLE BEASTS

Antelope, armadillo, bat (tastes like mouse, only mousier), coypu, donkey, elk, elephant, giraffe, guinea pig, goat, iguana, hedgehog, hippopotamus, llama, monkey, rhinoceros, seal, squirrel, zebra. Also horses, cats and dogs.

7

CHARCUTERIE

IT is debatable whether *charcuterie* should be included in a book mainly concerned with luxury foods. In France, Germany or Italy, *charcuterie* would certainly not be considered as a luxury, there being several *charcutiers* in every town and village of those countries, but here pork butchery, as it is termed, is a rare trade and the products are either sold in the not-too-abundant delicatessens who do not manufacture themselves, or in Soho where two or three pork butchers successfully cater for those palates which are not altogether satisfied with the ordinary British banger.

The word *charcuterie* serves for both the shop in which the product is sold and the product itself.

Charcuterie is the art of preparing meat, pork in particular, in as many different ways as possible, preserving it at the same time.

The Romans, as with so many other foods, were the first to elaborate on the art of pig-eating, since which time Italy has remained the foremost country producing the most interesting forms of *charcuterie*.

The curing of meat was carried out in 200 B.C. and the methods used in those days, as recorded by Cato, differ very little from present day practices.

The art of pork butchery travelled throughout Europe

with the Romans and reached its peak of popularity in the Middle Ages. In France in 1476 *charcutiers* came into their own and obtained a monopoly of selling cooked or raw pork meat, though they were not allowed to slaughter and had to buy the pork from other butchers. A pig, when dead, becomes pork. In the sixteenth century the *charcutiers* obtained the rights to kill and have been 'going the whole hog' ever since.

Success in smoking, salting and drying meats has been achieved over the years by a process of trial and error. Preservation must stop the growth of unwanted bacteria, or at least delay the growth, and yet not kill off the essential goodness in the food. Smoking is one way of preserving, the tars and acids in the smoke helping to counteract the formation of moulds.

Rubbing the surface of meat with a mixture of salt, salt-petre and sugar, then bedding it down in the same mixture, making sure that the surface is always in contact with the salt, is another form of preservation. So is immersion in a salt solution containing twenty-five per cent salt or the introduction of a brine into the meat by injection with a hollow needle.

The ham is probably the most taken-for-granted product of *charcuterie* and the majority of people would not consider it as anything very special in the way of food, but there are countless varieties of ham. The most popular is the cooked York ham, now canned, or sold ready sliced in polythene wraps so that it tastes nothing like the original. A real York ham is something very different from the pappy, salty, anaemic stuff that is passed off as ham in sandwiches. From Germany there are the Mainz,

Hamburg, Stuttgart and Westphalian hams, from Italy the Parma, from France the Bayonne, to name only the most famous.

The Bayonne and Parma hams are served raw, and though their seasonings differ, the basic production is the same. They are cut off the carcass in a traditional way by experts, the cut of the ham being of paramount import- ance. In the case of the Bayonne ham it is shaped like a 'Q' by the main joint being broken and the leg pressed to- wards the centre of the thigh bone.

The hams are salted by hand in a temperature of minus 2 degrees C., two below freezing. This takes two to three weeks, after which they are hung in a warm drying-room for three or four days, to sweat a little, then in a cooler dry- ing-room for at least three months.

The expense of these hams, they are roughly double the price of York hams, is due mainly to labour costs, for the men who salt the hams work in extremely unpleasant con- ditions, wearing fur-lined coats and hats to keep warm in the refrigerators and rubbing the coarse salt into the hams with their bare hands, which become, after years in their trade, as hard as leather and, no doubt, much saltier than the hams themselves.

Bayonne hams are strung up by threading a thick string through the skin of the ham at the angle of the joint. The Parma hams hang down from the leg.

These hams are served at the beginning of a meal as a dish by itself – not unlike smoked salmon, sometimes with a slice of melon. It is raw, salt meat, extremely delicate in taste and has the peculiarity of, if cooked, becoming quite uneatable, being both too tough and too salty.

Each ham weighs between 18 and 20 lb., and costs about £1 per lb.

Parma ham is now sold in tins, sliced, and though this naturally cannot be as good as the unpreserved hams, it is extremely good value for money. The tins, flat and round, contain either 6 or 12 oz. of sliced ham, the slices carefully separated by thin sheets of glazed paper. Cost 17s. 6d. for the 6-oz. tin, 28s. for the 12-oz.

For those who enjoy these types of raw salted meats, but find that buying a whole ham is a little embarrassing, there is an Italian product called *Coppa* which is much smaller and comes very near in taste to the Parma.

The *Coppa* is lean pork from the neck and shoulders of the pig, rolled into a cylindrical shape with salt, ground pepper and sugar rubbed into it. This seasoning follows a similar process to the raw hams, but white wine is poured over the rolled *Coppa* after it has been in the refrigerator about a week. Left to soak, the seasoning is rubbed in it again then it is strung tightly, to make the cylinder solid, sheathed in a large sausage skin and strung tightly again like a salami. The *Coppa* hangs in a cool drying-room for some three months before it is ready to eat.

Salamis, though commonplace enough in delicatessens and serving as main decoration to most Italian shops in Soho, are not just ordinary sausages dried and wrapped in silver paper as some people seem to think.

Salami sausages are made in many countries but the main producers originally were the Italians. Bologna and Milan are the big names; from France comes the Strasbourg, and the Hungarians also make a good one.

There is no one method of making salami, every country and every manufacturer has his own recipe. The principles, however, are the same. A salami can contain only pork meat or pork with a certain percentage of beef. Whatever the proportions are, the meat is first of all chopped finely. The chopping is done by machine while the meat is still frozen, after having been in the refrigerator for this purpose – hard meat chops up better than soft.

White pork fat is treated in a similar way, chopped in slightly larger cubes, then mixed with the lean meat together with salt, pepper, spices and sugar.

Once all the ingredients have been mixed together the resulting mass is pushed, by filler machines, into large sausage skins, some two to three inches in diameter and twelve to fifteen inches long.

These skins are then strung. The stringing is an important operation, for it is the tightness which forces the meat inside the skin into a compact mass. A very fine string is used and the work of winding and knotting requires time and skill.

Once the salami has been strung it is hung in various drying-rooms which vary in temperature and moisture. The process of drying and changing from one room to another takes two to three months, depending on the recipe.

Salami is always served in hors d'œuvres, and is eaten as a first course by itself with bread and butter. It should be cut into fine slices, the skin around the slice being removed. It is also used extensively in sandwiches.

Prices vary with the quality of the product, but a Milan salami can cost anything up to 15s. per lb. The Danes make a very commercial salami for as little as 5s. per lb., the average salami weighing between $1\frac{1}{2}$ and 3 lb.

Among other well-known Italian *charcuterie* products is the *mortadella*. This is a large type of sausage, weighing up to ten pounds and shaped like a rugger ball. Unlike salami or *coppa* it is cooked pork meat.

Its manufacture dates back to the Middle Ages when it was made with pork meat which was still warm, the pig having been slaughtered only minutes before.

Now this idea of speed seems less essential, but the recipe has not changed at all. The pork meat is finely minced and mixed with large cubes of white pork fat – about a square centimetre – the mixture is then pushed into ox bladders and strung carefully, though less elaborately than salamis.

The *mortadella* is then cooked, by boiling, hung up to dry for a few days, then is ready to be eaten. Served as an hors d'œuvre it is sliced and eaten like ham.

As we live in the great plastic age where nothing naturally good must be allowed to survive, for reasons which can only be commercial, it is sad to see that even continental foods are being subjected to synthetic treatment wherever possible. One of the most ludicrous inventions is the artificial sausage casing.

Ever since the Assyrians poured pigs' blood into a pig's intestine, cooked it and called it Black Pudding, the gut of pig, sheep or cow has been used for encasing sausages. As the average pig has four yards of small intestine and twelve yards of large intestine inside him and all this can be used to good purpose, it seems extraordinary that it has been found necessary to imitate this very natural product in plastic. However, cleaning guts is an unpleasant business, and artificial casings cause no one any trouble, except the poor customer who has to pretend very hard that what he is eating is delicious. Natural products should always be used where food is concerned; to present one with a sausage in plastic is madness. Certainly to pretend that salamis sheathed in printed synthetic casings are good is carrying pretence too far. The meat cannot sweat, breathe or even dry properly. But the day will come, no doubt, when we will all have the pleasure of consuming an all-plastic *andouillette*.

The *andouillette* is made of chitterlings – and chitterlings are pigs' guts. It is a French dish originating from the northern towns of Caen and Cambrai.

The pigs' intestines are first thoroughly cleaned in hot water and scraped to remove any dirt or grit. They are slit down the middle and spread flat on a table, sprinkled with salt, pepper and other seasoning, depending on the *charcutier*'s own recipe. These lengths of seasoned intestines are then pulled through a larger intestine, and the resulting long sausage is poached for a period of seven hours. It is then laid out to cool, and cut into sections of six inches in length. These sections are the *andouillettes*.

Andouillettes are usually grilled and served with mashed potatoes, but are excellent *à la Lyonnaise*, or *à la Strasbourgeoise*.

As *andouillettes* are a speciality they are rare, they have to be made to order and this is why they fall into the category of luxury – but they are not at all expensive, maybe 4s. per lb., a pound containing six to eight *andouillettes*.

8

BIRDS

IN days of old when knights were bold, the peacock was a very important bird. In the Middle Ages it not only held pride of place at banquets, but somehow managed to make the bravest of men believe it had magic powers. Before leaving for some dangerous dragon-infested land, to win a fair damsel in distress, a knight invariably took an oath on the peacock, and if he failed to carry out his promises it was a bit of a blot on his escutcheon.

During a banquet thrown in his honour, the knight would lay his hand on the side of the platter that the peacock was placed on, and swore in trembling voice with such sacred words as 'I vow to God, the Holy Virgin, Ladies and the Peacock to accomplish my mission,' and so on . . .

This vow was taken amid the praises and applause of the more intelligent noblemen who wouldn't think of venturing forth, but who, all the same, were very pleased to have yet another opportunity of devouring a few morsels of the tasty bird.

The peacock was presented *en volaille*, that is skinned, roasted, then re-decked in all its plumage. The beak and feet were usually gilded, and from its open mouth flames could be seen to shoot out – simply a matter of lighting a piece of alcohol-soaked cotton-wool placed there for the purpose.

Carried in solemn procession to the high table, it was carved by the noble knight, if he was skilful enough. It was not so much a matter of knowing how to use the knife as being able to calculate exactly how big a portion each guest could have, for everyone had to have a piece of the vowed-upon bird, and sometimes the banquets were thrown for several hundred people.

The twentieth century being less chivalrous, peacocks have gone out of fashion except at the odd eccentric's dinner. A young bird is worth the eating, however, if you get the chance, tasting a little like pheasant though a trifle more oily.

A dead peacock is the same price as a live one, the cost of which will depend on its health, age and plumage. Hens are no good, not really being presentable; cocks are rarer. The cheapest way to get one is to buy an egg and hope it'll hatch, under a chicken, but this is doubtful.

Swans, just as majestic, are easier to get hold of, but certain laws make them prohibitive for eating. Cygnets, however, are eaten once a year in a historical ceremony in the City of London. The smoking-hot birds are brought into the dining-hall in large pewter dishes carried by the chefs, heralded by gaily costumed musicians playing a traditional air.

All this beautifully decorative occasion, with its pomp and history, cannot, however, alter the fact that the swan does not make good eating. Not only is it oily, but leathery too. They'd be better off with a bit of chicken.

Bird fanciers no longer have much say in the preparation of menus today, but in the sixteenth century things were very different, birds were very much appreciated.

At a banquet given to Catherine de Medici by the City of Paris in 1549, 30 peacocks, 21 swans, 33 pheasants, 13 partridges, 9 storks, 33 turkeys, 33 flamingoes, 33 geese, 80 spring chickens, 90 quail, 99 pigeons and 99 doves were consumed.

Probably the most popular of wild birds in this country is the PHEASANT, a resident bird. There are three varieties, the common pheasant, the golden and the silver. Between twenty and thirty inches long, the pheasant is very decorative, having neck feathers shot with blue, his body chestnut brown marked with cream, black, iridescent green and purple, and having two ear tufts behind his featherless red head.

Though the cock is the more beautiful, the hen is better to eat. Pheasants should not be plucked too soon after being shot, as the unplucked bird keeps its aroma longer, the oil in the feathers preventing air getting at the flesh, and seeping back into the meat, making it all the more tasty.

Game birds can be excellent, but the right time must be chosen to eat them. A lot can be lost by not eating them at the *bon moment* and, epicures maintain, the *bon moment* is when the pheasant is on the point of decomposing.

The PARTRIDGE, a much smaller bird, only about twelve inches long, is nearly as popular as the pheasant. Also a resident in this country, it lives on cultivated land, rises with a whirring sound at the approach of a gunman, is chestnut brown with a sandy head, grey neck and breast with a chocolate horseshoe on the belly and has the great advantage of being plump. The partridge originates from Italy. The King of Naples brought several pairs to France when the Borgias were living it up and, following the fashion, they multiplied till they occupied most of Europe.

A real edible native in this country is the GROUSE. Grouse are fifteen inches long, glossy black with lyre-shaped tails and white underparts. The hen, to be different, is mottled brown. That is the black grouse. The red grouse is a dark mottled red with black underparts, and is easily recognizable by the rather ugly red combs over its eyes. The legs of grouse are not usually served as the whole bird has a taste of pine, not loved by everyone, and most of this taste is concentrated in the legs. It is best roasted.

The best winged game bird is the WOODCOCK. It should be eaten when extremely high even if this gives you indigestion. When alive, the woodcock, a thirteen and a half inch long resident, is brown and chestnut with black bars, a long thin bill and a high forehead. Wisely it remains under cover by day.

For those who live in the country, or who live in towns and dream of living in the country, the following is a quick guide to edible birds which are rarely served in restaurants because they are hard to come by, but which can easily be shot at with a little practice. It should be remembered, however, that Britain is an animal-loving country and many birds are protected, and those which are not completely protected are given long holiday periods, known as 'close season'.

You must not, for instance, shoot and eat blackbirds,

bustards, herons, lapwings, larks, quail or swans. With others you may indulge.

Normally you should *not* 'draw' birds that have slender tapering beaks or long slender beaks, and small game birds should always be eaten fresh, also undrawn, while, as they say, the gun is still smoking.

The LARK has a delicate flesh but is popular in some countries as a pet because it sings so well. Due to this it is sometimes a *faux pas* to offer it to guests – specially sentimental females. Larks' tongues were a great delicacy at Roman banquets, eaten by the spoonful, but lark *pâté* is favoured in France as the best way of presenting this bird. It is about seven inches long and has brown and white feathers.

The LAPWING, a resident bird, is also known sometimes as the green plover or peewit. It is a graceful bird with iridescent glossy plumage, black, white and a bit of brown. Twelve inches long, it lives in marshes and mud-flats and is recognizable by its crested head. Delicate flavoured meat.

The QUAIL is a bird of passage and only seven inches long. Plump, brown, like a miniature partridge, it lives in fields and wastes. It should never be allowed to get high.

The SNIPE, half the size of a woodcock, will fly away from you in a zig-zag pattern, just as you fire at it. Dark and light brown with conspicuous stripes on crown and back, it stays hidden in marshes by day. A resident.

The THRUSH is lovely when roasted and served on fried bread, but it is best not to boast about eating it as it is be-friended by most housewives who feed it breadcrumbs on winter mornings.

TURTLE DOVES should not be eaten in hotels reputed for honeymooners. They have black markings on a chestnut back, pinkish head and underparts with a few black and white stripes on light grey flanks. They are eleven inches long and visit the British Isles between May and October. They coo beautifully to each other and are very lovable – really a good example for the future.

GUINEA FOWLS are good to eat, though rather dry. Natives of West Africa, they were brought to England in the fifteenth century when they were known as turkeys, till real turkeys came along and put everyone right. When Shakespeare talks turkey, he really means guinea fowl.

Other than eating the birds, a great deal of pleasure can, of course, be had by consuming their eggs. Ostrich, turkey, goose, peacock and duck eggs are all bigger than the monotonous chicken's. Pigeon, guinea fowl, pheasant, partridge, lapwing, plover and gull are smaller. Duck and goose eggs are oily.

GROUSE are out of season from February to August.

PARTRIDGES from March to August.

PHEASANTS from March to September.

PIGEONS from March to October.

PLOVERS in April, May and December.

QUAIL in January, February, and from August to November.

SNIPE in April, May, July, August, and September.

WOODCOCK from May till August.

WILD DUCK from March to August.

LARKS are out of season except in October.

9

BIRDS' NESTS AND OTHER SOUPS

I F it wasn't for the fact that Chinese cookery, together with French cookery, is generally recognized by top gourmets as being the best in the world, one might hesitate to include birds' nests soup – a renowned Chinese delicacy – knowing it to be made only with a *consommé* base and bird spit. But epicures consider it a luxury and it is certainly not cheap.

Birds' nests soup is made with the nest of the Salanganes, wrongly called the sea-swallow. The nest is made by the bird dribbling lengths of sticky saliva one on top of the other till a font-shaped crust is formed against a rockface.

Just before the mating season, when the birds start nesting, their saliva glands swell considerably during digestion and produce a thick white liquid composed mainly of nitrogenous matter which is insoluble in water. It is this liquid that makes the nest.

The finding and collecting of these nests is extremely dangerous, as the Salanganes build them high up on precipitous rocks or in the walls of grottos overlooking the sea. They only exist along the Annam coast in Java, and also on some of the other islands off Malaya. The high price paid tempts natives to search for them, and the risks they have to take puts the price up.

Once the nests have been collected they are rinsed in hot water several times before being rubbed with groundnut oil. The oil helps to unstick feathers and any other dirt which might have collected in the nest. They are then rinsed again to remove the oil and packed in tins in much the same way as biscuits.

Before being used in soups they have to be soaked in cold water for two hours. In the water they swell and become transparent. They are then blanched for five minutes, drained and put in a boiling clarified chicken or beef stock. The soup is then kept on the boil for at least forty-five minutes.

During the cooking the nests fall to pieces, the thin gelatinous layers separate and the substance which held these filament-like layers together gives the soup its characteristic viscous texture.

It is believed that the sticky substance produced by the birds, that keeps the hardened filaments of saliva together, comes from the seaweed on which the birds feed. So-called swallows' nests have been sold in Europe which are not nests at all but man-made copies constructed with agar-agar – a jelly prepared from seaweed.

Birds' nests soup, or *Consommé au Nids d'hirondelles*, should always be served in a cup.

Nests weigh approximately a quarter of an ounce each and are sold by weight at about £1 per oz.

In England, traditionally, TURTLE SOUP is the aristocratic soup which is held in the highest esteem, served at great ceremonial banquets, diplomatic dinners and sometimes on Royal occasions. It is considered to combine the two essential qualities for a good soup – delicate taste and valuable nourishment. If, however, in previous chapters the reader has found that foreigners are apt to put their stomachs before the animal's feelings, it might be well to dwell a little on this all-English recipe.

How many, who dip their silver spoons into the clear, hot, sticky, sherry-tanged liquid, have asked themselves how a turtle is killed? The problem, on the face of it, seems to be the same as the lobster's, except that a rather larger saucepan might be needed to boil a turtle.

Turtles measure anything up to four feet in length and three feet in width, and the truth of the matter is that turtles are hanged.

They arrive alive in this country from South America, Africa, the West Indies and Australia, and are taken to the kitchens where the soup is to be made. They are put down in a corner somewhere and watched over by an apprentice chef, whose sole job it is to call out 'action stations' the moment he sees one of the turtles move. The sport is to wait till the turtle pokes its head out from beneath its shell and either lasso it or hook it by the chin.

If this is achieved successfully the turtle is hanged from a suitable scaffold, not to kill it, but to get the beast to expose enough neck so that its throat can be cut. It sounds barbarous, but in the end it's kindness itself.

The turtle, having been told by friends what may happen to it, does not help in any way and, being unbelievably strong and stubborn, can stay hanging for three or four days before its sheer weight exhausts it and obliges it to give up the struggle. When at last it exposes its leathery neck, an experienced slaughterer quickly flicks a razor-sharp knife in the right direction, after which everyone relaxes and thinks of soup.

Once the animal is dead no time is lost. Experts, equipped with hammers, chisels, saws and pliers get down to dismantling the beast, for getting the meat from the turtle is similar to decarbonizing an engine. A heave here, a pull there, the top comes off, then the bottom, then the flippers, and so on.

The top and bottom shells are cut, or sawn, into easily managed pieces, and, with the flippers, boiled till the meat can be easily removed. The meat is then blanched for a few minutes, put in a stew pan with a specially-prepared richly-flavoured *consommé*, vegetables and herbs, and cooked for about seven hours.

The better pieces of meat are removed from the soup before they are overcooked and cut into small pieces. The soup, when ready, is then strained and reheated. Basil, marjoram, sage, rosemary, savory, thyme, coriander and pepper are added, a good dollop of sherry or madeira poured in and, once finally stirred, the soup is ready to eat.

In each plate two small pieces of the previously cut turtle meat are served and, piping hot, it is placed before the guests.

Turtle soup is preserved and sold by most high-class grocers in tins or in bottles. The sizes vary, but the price is usually about 5s. per pint.

Turtle meat from the flippers can be eaten as a separate dish; the flesh of the terrapin (land turtle) is also edible though not considered particularly delicate.

Due to transport difficulties, dry turtle meat is imported in great quantities for the making of turtle soup. The animals are killed by the natives who fish for them, and the meat is laid out in the sun to dry. When dry it is as hard as teak and quite unbreakable. It has to soak for two or three days before becoming soft.

All along the south coast of France chefs are busy in their kitchens competing in producing the best recipe for BOUILLABAISSE. This competition has been going on for years and years. In any Mediterranean town you will find several restaurants advertising their *bouillabaisse*, nowhere is it quite the same, and if you like fish soup this particular one has the added advantage of surprise. You never know what you may find in it.

The true *bouillabaisse* originates from Marseille, and for the soup to be called a *bouillabaisse* at all, it must have certain fish in it.

Angler fish, chapon, conger eel, crabs, crawfish, red mullet, rouquier, Saint Pierre, sea perch, whiting are essential. If, however, these are unobtainable, which they may well be if you live in England, acceptable substitutes are recommended: grayling, gurmet, mackerel, perch, pike, trout, tunny and turbot.

Chopped and seeded tomatoes with chopped onions are first cooked in oil at the bottom of a large casserole. All the crustaceans are then dropped in, the hard fish, then the softer fish. To these are added pounded garlic, parsley, thyme, bay leaf, orange peel, cloves, salt, pepper and saffron. Water and more olive oil are added and the whole lot cooked.

Bouillabaisse is served in a large soup plate on top of bread – good, freshly baked crisp bread – *not* toast or fried bread.

On no account allow any *restaurateur* to serve you with a *bouillabaisse* containing mussels. This is considered to be an insult to its originator.

Bouillabaisse is now available in tins for home consumption. A pint tin sells at about 5s.

Another fish soup which is more common and now successfully preserved in tin is the BISQUE D'HOMARD – or cream of lobster soup. This simple recipe contains lobster, butter, white wine, brandy, rice, fish stock, fresh cream, thyme, bay leaf, salt, pepper and cayenne pepper. A pint tin sells at about 4s.

OCTOPUS SOUP, as yet uncanned, is another adventure in fish eating. Though this dish is not always served as a soup and is sometimes known under the label of *Poulpe Provençale*, the quantity of liquid served with the dish makes it eligible for this chapter.

The Greeks have been eating octopus for centuries and it is still one of their traditional dishes.

The tentacles, cut up, and the middle of the creature, with eyes and mouth removed, are cooked in oil with a liberal helping of chopped onions. Half a bottle of white wine is added and the contents of the ink bag emptied, giving the soup its characteristic strong flavour and black looks.

Tentacles, dried in the sun, cut into tiny pieces and cooked over charcoal are also served as an appetizer. The important thing to remember about octopus, whichever way you intend eating it, is that the flesh must be softened. In the kitchen this is done by beating the dead animal with a stick; the Greek fishermen, however, usually test their strength by bashing the creatures against the rocks. When just caught they have the resilience of a squash ball.

Leaving the sea, an Australian dish has made its way to the gourmet's table in recent years in the form of KANGAROO TAIL SOUP.

Whether this is more interesting than delicious is a matter of taste, but its popularity is fast increasing.

There are two kinds of kangaroo tail soup, thick and clear. The long thick tail used as a support by the animal when standing on its hind legs, or hopping, is skinned and boned. The meat is then stewed with carrots, leeks and onions for about half an hour. The whole is then covered with a meat stock and cooked for a further three hours.

Once strained, and garnished with pieces of cooked kangaroo tail meat, carrots, turnips and celery, it is flavoured with sherry and served.

Kangaroo tail soup is available in tins. About 4s. 6d. a pint.

10

SNAILS AND FROGS

Hunting, shooting and fishing – the recognized Englishman's sports. The sports of the leisured classes, the sports of the hungry poacher. Painted, sung about, eulogized, the chasing of the deer, the shooting of the pheasant, the hooking of the trout, all have had their fair share of artistic praise. But what of the two greatest sports of all – the hunting of the snail and the catching of the frog? Few sports are so exciting and require such skill.

It is summer, but pouring with rain. Your nose is pressed against the window pane as you count the seconds between the flashes of lightning and the booms of thunder. Soon, you hope, the rain will stop, and eventually it does.

Shod in light gumboots, you venture out into the sopping garden and walk in the long grass you have failed to mow for weeks. That is where they will be.

The air is warm, the vegetation humid, the atmosphere tropical, the blades of grass sparkling with the drops of rainbow rain when suddenly, quite suddenly, you catch sight of the tell-tale silvery trail.

It is not too easy to see in the grass, but soon it leads to a path and there, in the middle, heading at speed for your favourite and only vine, is the lovely plump snail.

Cautiously, lest it should hear you, you creep up behind it and dexterously pick it off the ground. The first of two dozen with which you will amuse your palate in a few weeks' time.

This, of course, is not a sport people in every country can indulge in. There are snails and snails, but England was rich in them once, a long time ago.

In a book called *The Wild Foods of Great Britain – Where to Find Them and How to Cook Them*, published before the 1914 war, Mr Cameron, the author, asserted that the French edible snail was introduced by the Romans and that it was plentiful on the South Downs and on the Cornish coast headlands. In Gloucestershire many tons of garden snails, he says, were collected annually in the south Cotswold district and sent into Bristol where they were commonly eaten by the working classes, especially by the employees in tobacco factories.

So much for the perverse English disdain of foreign gasteropod molluscs.

Snails as food were first mentioned in the Latin Bible by Moses, forbidding them as a meat.

Later Aristotle talked of a snail spoon with a pointed end specially designed to pick out the animal from its shell. Pliny tells of Romans consuming vast quantities and speaks in his *Natural History* of one, Fulvius Hirpinus, who in 49 B.C. started the first snail parks for breeding purposes and imported snails from all over the world. Also of Roman vessels coming regularly with quantities of the beasts from Sardinia, Sicily, Capri, and Spanish and African coasts.

In the parks the snails were fattened with wheat flour and aromatic plants and were regarded as helpful to the digestion. Thoughtful hosts would serve them at the end of typically endless Roman meals and they were also said to be helpful in the reviving of people with hangovers.

In Roman Gaul the tradition was handed down and banquets ended with hot or cold tarts, various cakes, white cheeses, honey, fruit and finally grilled snails.

After the fall of the Roman Empire snails became less popular but were eaten by everyone during religious fasting periods. The snail, being regarded as lean meat, was acceptable to monks and nuns who started breeding the little animals.

Their popularity went up and down, however. In 1393 a book entitled *Ménagier de Paris* says that snails were only for the very rich. Rabelais, later, said it was anybody's food, again mentioning fasting periods.

In the seventeenth century Charlotte Elizabeth of Bavaria (Louis XIV's sister-in-law) astonished her Court by eating quantities of snails and declaring them 'in', thus setting a new fashion. But Diderot in his encyclopaedia (1765) said that only peasants ate snails, in stews and soups. Snails obviously lost prestige.

In 1814 they came back into favour when the Prince de Talleyrand offered Alexander the First, Tsar of Russia, snails at a banquet, and during the famine of 1816 they were eaten by necessity and were found to be so good that their popularity from then on never looked back.

From a medicinal point of view the mucus of snails was said to be excellent for curing nose bleeds, and when crushed with oil and boiled the resulting mess spread over burns was said to act as a great soother. The eating of them was also believed to be useful for women in labour, and in the *Nouveau Dictionnaire d'Histoire Naturelle* of 1817, snails boiled and prepared in some special way were recommended as a beauty treatment for young women with spots.

All this, however, does not alter the fact that snails, if not carefully processed before eating, are highly dangerous. Though the snail itself is not poisonous, the food it eats is, and can result in a very unpleasant bout of colic or slow, agonizing death. While human beings enjoy eating snails, snails enjoy eating wartwort, henbane and deadly nightshade.

If allowed to, snails will live for five years. They come out of hibernation in April after seven months of deep sleep. From then on they wake up early every morning, before the sun is too hot, to have their meal of the day. They eat very slowly, but very regularly, never ceasing to munch like a machine in perpetual motion.

Once fed, they find a shady spot and doze the rest of the day away. They do not like heavy rain or wind, and when there is a drought they go into temporary hibernation pulling themselves back in their shells and secreting a mucus which seals the entrance with a hard veil.

In September they start eating later and later each day, the sun being less hot, and, though healthy, behave as though they were lacking in vitamins. Eventually they nuzzle themselves a small hole in the ground with their snouts, drop in, turn round so that they face the sky, seal up their shells with a hard white enamel-like mucus and go to sleep.

Snails are hermaphrodites. They lay eggs in deep holes, eighty or ninety at a time, depending on their species, which after a month come out as tiny snails.

There are two types of edible snail, the *bourgogne* and the *petit gris*.

The *bourgogne* is the more colourful of the two, and the larger, having alternate brown and white stripes running perpendicularly to the apex of the shell. The *petit gris*, as the name implies, is smaller and all grey.

The snail's body has two parts, the top part sheathed anti-clockwise in the shell, and the bottom part, or foot, with the head which has two long horns and two short ones, the longer to see with, the shorter to feel.

Beneath these horns there is a mouth, with leathery teeth, and all the other organisms are placed along the right of its body.

The shell is all in one piece like a long narrow cone curled three or four times on itself. The wall of the *bourgogne* is doubled and hollow, the wall of the *petit gris* is solid. The shells are wound clockwise from the centre, which is projected to the right.

In some species, found mainly in central Europe, there are left-sided snails, with all their organs on the left, the shell wound anti-clockwise and the centre projected to the left. These are not edible.

Once picked, the snail must be starved before being consumed so that any of the poisonous foods it may have eaten are completely cleared from its digestive system. This may take up to a fortnight. Sometimes the snails are starved, then fed on fattening foods and starved again so that, in the end, the snail is plumper.

The quickest and kindest method of killing the snail is by dropping it into boiling water.

Though there cannot be any proof of this, it is believed

that death is instantaneous, the shock alone taking its breath away – for ever.

If the water is heated gradually to save it some hardship, the animal will come out of its shell and die peacefully enough, but then it will be quite impossible to re-curl it and put it back in the shell. It must, therefore, always be dropped into bubbling hot water.

Once dead, and removed from its shell by means of an instrument similar to a crochet hook, the snail is rinsed thoroughly. The shell is also cleaned, separately, boiled in soda water, then thoroughly washed and rinsed.

Bourgogne snails are cooked, in a *court bouillon*, for any-thing between 1½ and 3 hours, depending on their size; *petit gris* for 25 to 40 minutes. Once cooked they are left to cool in the *court bouillon* so that they can retain all the flavour of their own juices and those of the herbs.

At this stage the snails are ready for consumption. If they are to be preserved, they are packed in tins, 24 to the tin, which are sold, together with 24 shells, in boxes or poly-thene bags.

In France, where the consumption is greater than in this country, snails are sold fresh in markets every day. These are ready buttered and presented in cardboard boxes. In England large quantities are imported in tins, and the majority of restaurants use these as they are most econo-mical. There is very little difference between the preserved and the fresh snail, as it is, after all, the taste of the garnish that matters more than the taste of the animal itself.

For the simplest recipe – *Escargot à la Bourguignonne* – the empty shells are first filled with a little garlic butter, the snails themselves are pushed in, the shells are sealed with more butter. The filled shells are then sprinkled with fresh breadcrumbs and heated for ten to fifteen minutes in the oven.

Garlic butter, or *escargot* butter, is simply a mixture of butter, garlic, shallots, salt, pepper and parsley in certain proportions. Some chefs add shredded coconut, or crushed almonds, or a few drops of lemon juice, and some even add a dose of pernod for good measure.

Snails should be served with a white wine if eaten at the beginning of the meal. A Champagne, Arbois, Muscadet, a dry Graves, a Saint Péray, a Riesling, Sylvaner or Tokay d'Alsace.

If the snails are to be the main dish, and each guest is going to consume a large quantity, then a red wine should be served – a Châteauneuf du Pape, or a Côtes du Rhône. A Cabernet, Rosé d'Arbois or Tavel are also quite acceptable.

Boxes, containing 24 snails in tin and 24 shells, are retailed at high-class grocery stores for about 12s. 6d.

Escargot butter, specially prepared and enough for 24 snails, costs about 4s. 6d. per jar.

And what of the other sport – the catching of frogs?

This requires far more skill than snail-hunting, and ingenuity for making the special, weatherproof, soundproof frog gun. The gun should be a device capable of shooting a small harpoon in the direction of the frog, the harpoon having a long length of string attached to it.

Another piece of equipment necessary, even more vital than the harpoon, is a long thin stick on the end of which is dangled a small red flag.

Crouching among the reeds near a pond where you have heard frogs singing to each other the night before, you should wave the little red flag to attract their attention. Frogs, like bulls, are puzzled by little red flags and will pop out of their hiding places to have a closer look. That is when you fire your harpoon and retrieve your catch. (There is no truth in the rumour that bull-frogs are called bull-frogs because they get angry when seeing red.)

If you do not like the idea of using a small harpoon, or are honest enough to admit that you may not be too good a shot, excellent results are obtained with a large net. Frogs, it has been noticed, enjoy the sport much more with nets, as frog catchers are apt to smack the things down on to nenuphar leaves missing the frog and causing themselves to get very wet. Frogs have a sense of humour.

Once caught frogs have to be killed. This is done quickly by chopping their heads off. Once you've done that you chop their legs and feet off and discard everything but the *back* legs. That is all that is edible.

The little legs should then be threaded on to a skewer and immersed in very cold water for a long time, the water being changed at intervals to keep fresh. The effect of this cold water is to make the legs swell and grow whiter.

There are seventeen ways of preparing frogs' legs once you have got that far and hardly any of them are worth the trouble. The only recipe that may cause some embarrassment to Anglo-Saxon friends is *Grenouilles à l'Anglaise*, which can only mean that the English ate quantities of frogs along with snails long before they started insulting Napoleon.

Frogs' legs were very expensive to import, but now with

the help of science are available frozen. The freezing of the legs manages to remove the hardly existing taste, which makes them even less worthwhile, but for a giggle you will have to pay approximately 30s. for a dozen pairs. A dozen pairs is considered a fair portion.

There are many species of frogs, most of which can be found in this country. The small green frog which lives in areas known to be clean is the one to eat. Toads are not recommended.

11

TRUFFLES

THE truffle is a subterranean fungus the size of a golf ball, composed of water, carbohydrate, albumen, salt and fat. Its nutritive value is doubtful, its tight texture makes it indigestible, it is black, ugly, troublesome to find, impossible to cultivate but costs between 30s. and £2 the ounce.

It is the most expensive natural food in the world and its one redeeming feature is its unique and remarkable aroma. Place a truffle on a dozen new-laid eggs and twenty-four hours later all the eggs will taste of truffle.

There are several varieties of these 'black diamonds', as they are called by chefs, but the best and only ones worth considering are the *Truffes du Périgord*. These are found in two districts of France, Quercy-Périgord and Vaucluse-Gard – the former covering an area due east of Bordeaux, the latter due north of Marseille.

Some truffles are found in Dordogne, Burgundy, and Normandy, and the white truffles, which are more peppery and have a slight flavour of garlic, are collected in northern Italy around the Piedmont district.

In England, a variety has been found with no aroma at all, which is, however, edible, and, in olden times, truffle-hunting was a recognized pastime. The late Lord Winchelsea employed trained hogs, muzzled, to hunt for truffles over the chalk lands of Kent, and during the war truffled dishes served in some Soho restaurants were the outcome of exhausting excursions to Epping and Hainault.

Known for more than two thousand years, the origin of the truffle has been much debated. Juvenal and Plutarch both thought it was a substance formed in the ground by the effect of lightning heating up water and certain minerals when it struck in certain areas, while Dioscorides, a disciple of Isocrates, thought the truffle was just a tuberous root.

After the fall of the Roman Empire truffles were forgotten till the fourteenth century when they started appearing at the dinner-tables of the rich Italian and French nobility. Eclipsed again during the religious wars, they finally made the grade for ever when Louis XIV's chefs were inspired to invent more and more elaborate dishes to use them, when they discovered the power of their aroma.

In 1810, a peasant, by name Joseph Talon, living in the district of Vaucluse, found some truffles in a field where he had planted some acorns ten years before. Being a mean and cunning man, he said nothing of this to anyone, but experimented quietly and discovered that wherever oak trees grew in his area truffles were to be found. He started building up a big trade.

As he got old he bragged of his money-making discovery, and another gentleman, Auguste Rousseau, far more honourable and with nothing but his country's prestige at heart, set to work to cultivate the truffle and, at the Universal Exhibition of 1855, presented large specimens, which he had produced by planting acorns in certain types of soil.

Truffles, then already commanding a high price, became the cultivator's dream – and everyone went mad and planted oak trees everywhere in the Provence, Poitou and Périgord districts.

Unfortunately, only time revealed that truffles did not necessarily grow where oak trees grew; they appeared near oak trees, but only when and where they chose. Joseph Talon, rubbing his hands, and Auguste Rousseau, with tears in his eyes, realized that they had just been very lucky with their experiments.

Years of study on the truffle has still not revealed why it grows where it does, or why it fails to grow where it might be expected.

Weather hazards are partially responsible for the character of this temperamental vegetable. It is known that the truffle needs a hot summer, that it needs good thunderstorms in June, July and August to help its development. It is known that even a light frost helps it to ripen, but that any constant temperature below 5 degrees C. makes it soft. Though some beds have yielded truffles for twenty-five years, they have done so erratically, and sometimes growth in seemingly reliable beds has stopped abruptly, never to produce again.

Iron is needed in a damp, soft soil, with calcium and other chemicals and, as land strata change continually, it is luck, not good management, that enables people to grow truffles at all.

There are quite a number of areas where truffles grow naturally, but the bulk sold and consumed come from plantations which were seeded with oaks successfully many years ago.

Large areas of south-west France specially planted, however, have also proved quite barren, and plantations being prepared now cannot be expected to show results for at least another decade, and should these prove unsuccessful, then the truffle industry might well disappear altogether, the truffle pricing itself right out of the market.

Truffles, when they do grow, are collected between December and March, but not without difficulty, for they are hidden some two or three feet underground. Man, however, has brought in the animal to solve this problem and trained pigs and dogs to do the finding for him – as it is all a question of smelling the truffle out.

Whereas the dog is trained to recognize the smell of the truffle, after which he will happily hunt for it, knowing his reward to be some tasty tit-bit, the pig has to be trained not to eat the truffle when it finds one, having a natural liking for the precious lump.

Farmers who prefer using pigs to dogs find that the female of the species has a keener sense of smell, but it may take two years to teach a sow not to gobble up the truffle as soon as it finds it.

On fine winter mornings one can enjoy a walk through the lovely oak forests listening to the happy snorting and grunting of contented sows, occasionally interrupted by the ranting and raging of a poor truffle-hunter, who has not been able to control his beast in time.

Some hunters, who have been at the game all their lives, manage to find the expensive delicacy without using pigs or dogs. By studying the ground around an oak tree and noting the bumps and cracks, they can tell whether truffles are beneath the ground or not. Also a certain type of fly lays its grubs in truffle ground and the sight of a cloud of these flies is a sure indication that money is near at hand.

All this buried treasure, as might be expected, is a magnet to pirates and crooks. Though truffle markets, which are open during the collecting season, are well watched over by officials of the government, and there are strict rules and regulations about type, size and weight of truffles to be sold, the greed of certain people has made them stoop incredibly low.

Truffles are bought fresh from the collector by truffle canners, some by housewives, but these are very much in the minority. When they can, the dishonest collectors add a few lumps of coal to a bag of truffles, or paint lumps of lead black, or stick a number of small truffles together with pins so that they look like a more valuable large truffle. Small stones are also stuck in the cracks to increase the weight.

In Italy, the land of the Piedmont white truffle, pirates are abounding. By ancient law any truffles found on private land must be shared with the landlord, but the Communists wish to have this practice abolished. It is now quite a serious political issue, and a campaign requesting legislation declaring truffle-hunting free is under heated discussion. Hordes of countrymen have found they can live quite happily off this hunting-of-the-truffle; and the good truffle areas of Perugia, Pesaro, and Macerata, being depressed areas, have found the sport an alternative to immigration.

The honest truffles, sold and bought under strict rules,

are sorted into four categories before reaching the general public.

The *whole brosées* – whole brushed truffle, washed and brushed by hand.

The *whole pelées* – whole peeled, washed and peeled, usually used in the preparation of *foie gras*.

The *morceaux*, pieces of truffles which have been broken in transit or in the collecting.

And *pelures*, which are the peelings of the *pelées*, mainly used to enrich sauces.

All four categories are sold fresh and in tins.

As far as the English consumer is concerned, the truffle may seem to be a bit of a puzzle. Held in the hand, it means nothing, a lump of coal is just as exciting, and even in a dish containing truffles it might not seem very essential, but if there is any uncertainty in the reader's mind as to its worth, a simple experiment can be made by tasting a sauce with truffles, and the same sauce without.

12

VEGETABLES AND FRUITS

IF you have ever had difficulty in deciding whether you are eating a vegetable or a fruit, the difference between the two is quite simple to remember. Vegetables are plants or parts of plants – the roots, the bulbs, the tubers, shoots, stems, leaves or flowers. Fruits are the ovaries of plants. The tomato is a fruit, so is the cucumber, the olive, the marrow, the aubergine, to name but a very few, which are commonly eaten as vegetables and therefore called vegetables.

There are quite a number of ordinary vegetables and fruits which are regarded as luxuries in this country because they have become rare, not because of their price, but simply because there is not the demand for them, yet many of them are far more interesting from a culinary point of view than the adored cabbage and respected bean.

ARTICHOKES, for instance, are not a luxury in France, but in England the demand is so small that they are difficult to get in any provincial town even in season. The artichoke is, after all, an extremely civilized thistle with a very gastronomic beginning. It was discovered in the sixteenth century by a clever French gourmet, who immediately saw in its then barbaric state the possibility of something really appetizing.

By careful cultivation and grafting today's Globe and

T - D

Crown artichokes were achieved, though it took many centuries to get them to the large grapefruit size they are.

There are now a number of varieties, the best known being the Large Green of Laon, the Large Camus of Brittany and the Green of Provence. There are some small varieties, the Florence and the Purple Venice, which, unlike the larger species, can be eaten whole. Another Italian artichoke is the Carciofini, a miniature artichoke which is preserved in olive oil and makes an excellent hors d'œuvre.

Rich in mineral salts, iron and iodine, artichokes are best, from the health point of view, when eaten raw, either with a _vinaigrette_ or with salt. Many people, however, find them too unpalatable in their natural state, so eat them boiled.

The artichoke is a complicated plant, the best part of which is the 'fond' or bottom. This is the part that is preserved in tins and sold in tall cylindrical cans, but much pleasure can be had by sucking at the base of all the petals, nearly as much as getting rid of the sticky beard, which has to be removed from the heart before eating.

Not to be confused with the globe artichoke is the Jerusalem artichoke or Topinambour, which has a strange if not altogether vital history.

A certain Claude de Launay, explorer and no relation to the author, went to Brazil in 1608 and found a curious bunch of savages who called themselves the Topinambour tribe. So interesting were these people from an anthropological point of view that he brought several live specimens back to Paris and exhibited them.

Only a year before, in 1607, someone else had brought over from America just as strange a vegetable which had been cultivated in Massachusetts and which everyone called Poire de Terre for want of a better name, and also because it looked a bit like a potato only uglier.

When Claude de Launay exhibited his Brazilian savages some card unkindly related their physiques to the Poire de Terre and from then on the vegetable was called a Topinambour – though the savages were never called Poire de Terre.

The fact that we, in England, call the tuber a Jerusalem artichoke has absolutely nothing to do with the French story. Jerusalem, however, is apparently derived from the Italian name Girasole, but why the Italians called the vegetable Girasole remains a mystery.

Jerusalem artichokes are warty, unattractive, potato-like tubers which taste sweet and a little bit like artichokes, but that is the only similarity. There are several varieties, white, red, and purple, each of which is as good as the others. They grow in any soil and are at their best in March and April. Treated like turnips they make an excellent change from the usual garden vegetables, and are frequently used in garnishes by chefs who know how to interest the palate.

ASPARAGUS is the only vegetable, indeed probably the only food, that can be eaten not only hot and cold – but tepid. Few people realize this and, frankly, as a discovery it may not cause a revolution, but it is a great help to exemplary hostesses and cooks who are burdened with those terrible people who are rude enough to sit down at the dinner-table late.

Asparagus was eaten in Ancient Greece, and though the Romans (Cato and Pliny) were obviously proud of their efforts in cultivating the vegetable it was later known to grow wild along the sea coasts of Great Britain as well as in Battersea and sixty acres of Mortlake – in 1792.

The asparagus plant has roots from which stem branches and leaves, but it is the shoots which rise directly from the roots between May and June and cut before they become too thick that are eaten.

There are a number of varieties, the best known being the French Argenteuil, which have thick stems and purple heads, the English Green which are, surprisingly enough, green, smaller, thinner, but renowned for their flavour, the Genoa, sometimes known as *Asperge Violette* because it is purple, and the most popular variety, the Lauris, an improved English Green grown mainly in the south of France for preserving.

Asparagus is difficult to cook because the tip is soft and tender and the base is hard. The right way is to stand them up in a deep saucepan half full of water so that two thirds of the vegetable are boiled while the tips are steamed. Under cooking is better than over cooking, as they are so delicate, and they should never be served with a strongly flavoured sauce.

In asparagus there are traces of sulphur which, though not immediately detectable to the olfactory senses, are strong enough to ruin a wine, unless the asparagus is served as a garnish, or with grated cheese. Wines therefore should be avoided.

Unlike artichokes or aubergines, asparagus is on sale pretty well everywhere in season.

The AUBERGINE is a relative of the tomato, but bears

no resemblance to it. Originating from Arabia, it travelled east to India and Asia, and in 1587 came to England. Now it is common in South America and Africa, where it is cultivated for export.

The English name of Egg Plant comes from the fact that a rarer of its species is white and looks exactly like a hen's egg. The most common aubergine, however, is long and purple and about the size and as subtle as a handy cosh.

It has a unique refreshing taste and water-melon-like texture. Generally treated like a tomato, it is eaten hot, or raw with salt or *vinaigrette*, or served as a garnish.

One of the more expensive fruits sold in England, and one which is extremely popular in America though considered a luxury, is the AVOCADO PEAR.

A native of Africa and the West Indies, this pear-shaped fruit has a shiny green skin, weighs from 6 oz. to 4 lb., but is usually at its best when about $\frac{1}{2}$ lb.

Cut in two, the large peach stone sized kernel is removed and replaced by a sauce *vinaigrette* or shrimps in mayonnaise.

The nut-flavoured flesh of the pear has the soft, oily texture of butter and is eaten raw. As a sweet it is delicious if soaked in rum for a day or two.

BAMBOO SHOOTS are probably the most fashionable exotic vegetable of the day. Eaten fresh in the Far East like asparagus, they only get to us in tins or frozen. The shoots are from the long bamboo canes with which public schoolboys are corrected, and can be extremely dangerous if not carefully prepared.

The shoots are covered with very fine but sharp hairs which, if not removed before cooking, may perforate your intestines. Bamboo shoots served in Chinese restaurants and preserved in tin are, however, perfectly safe.

GUAVAS occasionally appear on menus. They are wholesome, sweet tropical fruit mainly grown in the West Indies. There are a number of varieties, the white, red, green, raspberry, and bastard. The white guavas are the most popular and are as large as hens' eggs, with succulent juicy flesh.

The guava is locally made into jam and jelly, and guava cheese is a product made from the pulp of the guava after the fruit has been used for jam-making.

Another Eastern fruit, which is more commonly eaten in England, is the LYCHEE. This berry, the size of a large cherry, has a nut seed in the middle surrounded by white translucent flesh and a hard red, often warty, outer skin which peels off easily.

Extremely refreshing, the lychee is also eaten dry, like a prune, when the skin has turned black. In this state it is called a 'lychee nut', but is nothing much to shout about.

Peeled and stoned lychees are preserved in tin for export.

OKRA, unlike the lychee, is a cultivated product which seems to be getting less popular. It is a long, bean-like, regular, five-sided, cone-shaped fruit, eaten as a vegetable. Its taste is unique, if a trifle bitter, and it is full of seeds, which add to the pleasure of eating. Many dishes appeal to the palate because of their strange texture, and this is one of them.

Known abroad, generally, as gombos, in the West Indies and South America as quimbongos, in France as banias and internationally referred to as okra, they are, for some reason, called 'ladies' fingers' in England. Though possibly flattering to this not very attractive fruit, the name seems definitely insulting to ladies – unless they are gardeners and think it a compliment to have green fingers.

As a vegetable okra is used as a garnish, in soups and also pickled in curries. The seeds, when dried, are sometimes used as a substitute for barley.

The PALM tree, pictures of which immediately bring to mind exotically exciting adventures in Tangiers or damp holidays in Torquay, is a very versatile tree as far as the gastronome is concerned. It has fruit (dates), nuts (coconuts), terminal shoots (cabbage palm), the interior stem (sago), the sap (palm wine) and, of course, oil.

CŒUR DE PALMIERS, the terminal leaf of a species of cabbage palm, is eaten cold, sliced or whole, with a vinaigrette. *Cœurs de Palmiers* (Palm Hearts) are rarely seen nowadays, but are worth a try. They are preserved in tins, but not in great quantities.

PIMENTOS are more commonly referred to in this country as peppers. Originating in India and brought to Europe by the Spaniards, there are many varieties, all of different shapes and sizes and taste.

Some, like glossy green over-sized carrots, are soft and

hollow, tasting sweet, while others, similar in shape, are bright red, kinky, and will send you diving straight into a water butt with mouth open wide screaming for the fire brigade after one small bite.

There are yellow pimentos, and dark violet ones, even black ones – the last two growing mainly in Hungary. Spanish pimentos vary from green to yellow to red, and sometimes manage to be all three colours. They are large and round, the size of grapefruit, and hollow like soft empty leather pouches. Most of these are sweet but not all, and a careful tasting before use is advisable if the customers in a restaurant are not to be seen reeling around the tables emptying carafes of wine down their inflamed throats.

Pimento seeds when dried and ground become pepper. The red kinky type produces cayenne, the violet from Hungary paprika, and others, the various white and black peppers, we have in our cruets.

Of all the varied ways in which vegetables and fruit are presented, crystallized fruits probably give the most pleasure to the eye even if they do not appeal to everyone's taste. A basket of 'fruits confits', or a sweet decorated with glacé fruits, is sure to bring a gay splash of colour to the table.

The crystallization of fruit, as an industry, can be traced back to 1342 when documents in the small town of Apt, some sixty miles north of Marseille, recorded that the local *confiseurs* had the honour of supplying Pope Clement VI, then residing in Avignon, with crystallized and glacé fruits non-stop for ten years. He had a sweet tooth.

The industry spread and it is probable that Clermont-Ferrand was the first place to export these fruits to England, though the Apt packers captured most of the national trade.

There is a difference between crystallized and glacéd fruits, but both preparations call for infinite patience and considerable skill, as each fruit has to be treated individually the moment it is ripe, and not all fruit ripen at the same time.

First the fruit is washed, peeled, stoned, sliced if necessary and placed in an earthenware basin, then covered with a hot but weak syrup composed of sugar and glucose. If sugar alone were used the fruit would harden and become uneatable, but the addition of glucose ensures that it will remain soft and tender for months.

Twenty-four hours later the fruit and syrup are reheated and more sugar is added. This process is repeated till the fruit is saturated and cannot absorb any more. The natural moisture of the fruit has therefore been replaced with the syrup.

The glacé finish is produced by heating the saturated fruit with syrup to boiling-point, cooling and drying in special drying-rooms, then varnishing each individual fruit with a special edible varnish, giving it that rich, glossy appearance.

The crystallized finish is produced by dipping the saturated fruit once more in syrup, then passing it through a very hot oven. This quick-drying treatment hardens the sugar, giving the fruit that attractive frosted look.

MARRONS GLACÉS – glacé chestnuts – the most popular

of all glacé fruits, are prepared with selected chestnuts from France and Italy. These chestnuts are shelled, placed in special containers, quickly boiled so that the interior skin can be removed, peeled, then treated like other fruit.

Crystallized flowers and petals go through the same process, whole violets and roses being favourites, but acacia, pink and mauve lilac, lavender and mimosa are also in demand for decorating.

ANGELICA, the only crystallized vegetable, is unique because of its bright green colour. The stalk of this alpine plant, found between Lapland and Spain, is mainly cultivated in France, where it is also used for flavouring and liqueurs. Angelica is said to have been eaten in this country as a salad, and in Norway its roots are still used as a substitute for bread.

The process of crystallizing angelica stalks is the same as for all other fruits.

13

CHEESE

IT is said that there are over one thousand different cheeses in the world, maybe more. In France alone five hundred varieties can be listed. To complicate the life of those interested in the subject, countries copy each other's cheeses and, now that we are in the latter half of this gloriously synthetic century, processed cheeses, spread-type cheeses and cheese-type spreads add to the confusion.

Real cheeses, those which are individually made in relatively small quantities, come under one of five categories – hard, blue-veined, semi-hard, soft and cream.

Cheeses are made with cow's milk, goat's milk or ewe's milk in its pure state, skimmed, partly skimmed or enriched with cream.

Coagulation, curdling or clotting of the milk is the first step in cheese-making. This is induced either by the natural fermentation of the milk, by the addition of a vegetable or fruit juice, or by the adding of rennet, a coagulating agent.

Animal rennet is a substance found in the stomachs of calves, lambs and kids; vegetable rennet is a similar substance found in certain vegetables.

The curdling, the addition of other agents, the cooking, the moulding in wooden, tinplate, earthenware, and pottery moulds, or in osier baskets, the ripening in caves, in drying-rooms, in varying temperatures, the addition of spices, of liqueurs, all give the cheeses individuality. No two cheeses are ever quite the same, and in the list that follows the majority of the world's more famous cheeses are briefly described to help the consumer recognize them at a glance.

In England cheese is served at the very end of the meal, in France it is served before the sweet, usually after a salad.

The majority of cheeses can be eaten throughout the year, but the most famous Bel Paese, Camembert, Gorgonzola, Munster and Stilton, are regarded as winter cheeses – November to May. Pont l'Évêque should not be served in August.

Burgundy and Bordeaux wines are best for strong cheeses, otherwise it is a matter of taste. Acceptable are a Beaune, Chambertin, Clos de Vougeot, Hermitage or vintage port.

BAGNES (Swiss) – A very hard cheese which is eaten as a special dish and known as *Fromage à la Raclette*. The cheese is cut $\frac{1}{2}$-inch thick, toasted under a grill, and when it starts to melt is scraped off on to a slice of bread. It is not to be compared with Welsh Rarebit.

BEAUFORT (French) – A semi-hard yellow cheese from Savoy, weighing 15 lb. to 30 lb. Round, flat, with a light brown skin.

BEL PAESE (Italian) – A large round, flat cheese, creamy with a mild flavour, weighing about 5 lb.

BLEU D'AUVERGNE (French) – Made with cow's, goat's and ewe's milk, this is a tall, round cheese of the Roquefort type – blue-veined – matured in canvas.

BLUE DORSET (English) – A hard, white cheese with a

'Royal Blue' vein running through it. The particular mould which forms the vein running horizontally through the cheese is unique.

BONDON (French) – A soft cheese which is sweet compared to most, having 2 per cent sugar added. It is loaf-shaped, and 1½ to 2 inches in diameter.

BRIE (French) – A large, flat, round cheese, a foot or so in diameter and 1½ inches thick, weighing about 6 lb. Larger ones are made measuring some 22 inches across. It is a soft cheese which is fully ripe if it bulges when gently pressed with the flat of a knife but does not run. It has a reddish crust with patches of white and is light yellow inside.

BROCCIO (French) – Small and cylindrical in shape, it is a soft Corsican cheese made from goat's or ewe's milk and used in cooking as well as eaten plain.

CACHAT (French) – A special cheese made of ewe's milk, ripened with vinegar and eaten in an onion skin. It is popular in Provence where it is usually eaten with a Châteauneuf wine.

CAERPHILLY (English) – A whole milk cheese originally made in Wales, but now manufactured in the west country. Weighing between 8 and 10 lb. it is sold when only ten days old.

CAMEMBERT (French) – The most famous of French cheeses and so appreciated by connoisseurs that a statue of its inventor, a Madame Harel, stands in the village of Camembert. Round, 6 inches in diameter, an inch thick, this soft cheese should not be runny, though many people eat it when it is turning liquid. Its crust is a light orange with a few white streaks, its paste pale yellow.

CANTAL (French) – Drum-shaped with a hard, speckled,

light-brown crust, this is a hard cheese, which does not smell as strongly as its surprisingly sharp taste would suggest. The paste is pale yellow. It is made in two sizes, one 7 inches high and 7 inches in diameter, the other 12 inches high and 12 inches in diameter.

CHEDDAR (English) – A hard cheese and much imitated. Farmhouse Cheddar made in Somerset is the true Cheddar, which takes a year to mature. Large millstone-shaped.

CHESHIRE (English) – A hard cheese like Cheddar, but reputed to be the oldest cheese recipe in England. There are three types, the red, white and blue, patriotic to say the least. The red cheese is the same as the white only with a colorant added, the blue is an accidental cheese starting off as red then, for some chemical reason, turning blue. It is considered the best. Large millstone-shaped.

COTTENHAM (English) – A semi-hard, blue-moulded, double cream cheese, made in the Midlands. A foot or so in diameter, it is drum-shaped.

COULOMMIERS (French) – A soft cheese, round, about 1½ inches high and 7 inches in diameter. Its paste is snow white with a slightly darker crust.

CREAM CHEESE – Most countries have their own recipe. The English cream cheeses come from Devon and Cornwall. Cream is usually added to the milk before the coagulating agent is introduced.

DOUBLE GLOUCESTER (English) – A hard but crumbly cheese as large and as flat as a grindstone, needing some six months to mature. The single Gloucester is similar but smaller and whiter.

EDAM (Dutch) – A semi-hard cheese as famous as Dutch

bulbs and wooden clogs because of its shape and colour. Round, weighing about 5 lb., its outer skin is bright red, the paste itself dark yellow.

EMMENTHAL (Swiss) – A hard cheese, often mistaken for Gruyère, but with much larger holes. It is sold in this country in vast quantities, wrapped in vacuum-packed polythene wrappers, but has many imitators.

ÉPOISSES (French) – A soft, cylindrically shaped cheese sometimes pickled in local brandy and known as Époisses au Marc de Bourgogne – it is made in the Côte d'Or *département*. It is eaten over-ripe and sometimes runny, and left in cellars to ripen accordingly.

FROMAGE À LA PIE (French) – Made from skimmed milk and eaten fresh when the milk has curdled. This takes a day or two. It is seasoned with salt, pepper and chopped chives or eaten with sugar – according to taste. Cream is always added.

GÉROMÉ (French) – A semi-hard cylindrical cheese flavoured with aniseed or caraway seed. It takes four months to ripen in cellars and has a darkish red crust.

GEX (French) – A blue-veined cheese which is distinguishable from all other blue-veined cheeses by its extraordinary whiteness.

GORGONZOLA (Italian) – The most famous Italian cheese. Blue-veined, its uniqueness of taste is due to the way the milk is curdled and the time of the day at which the manufacturing process starts. There is a very subtle difference between morning and evening milk and gorgonzola is a mixture of these two. Its quality also depends on its curing, which is carried out in the famous curing houses of Milan.

GOUDA (Dutch) – A larger and flatter version of the Edam, semi-hard, similar in taste and texture.

GRUYÈRE (Swiss) – A hard cheese, pale yellow and honeycombed with small holes. The rapid fermentation of the curd causes bubbles which explode and become holes. There is no truth in the story that the holes are first placed in a container and the cheese paste poured over them.

HERVÉ (Belgian) – A soft, square cheese made in three qualities with partly-skimmed milk, cream and double cream. It is turned out in cubes wrapped in beer-steeped cloth and ripened in dark cellars.

LIMBURGER (German) – A semi-hard cheese flavoured with tarragon, chives and parsley. It is dried in the sun, and its crust is made non-porous by the addition of salt. Its smell invariably precedes its arrival. Also made in Belgium and Alsace.

MAROLLES (French) – A semi-hard, square cheese, 6 inches across, with a dark red crust and potent smell.

MUNSTER (French) – A semi-hard, round cheese, about 6 inches across and 2 inches high, flavoured with aniseed, with a dark orange crust.

PARMESAN (Italian) – The hardest cheese of all and generally used throughout Italy for grating. It is regarded as the correct cheese to use with pastas. With a black crust, the cheese is a pale straw colour with tiny little holes in the paste. When first cut a sticky substance, not unlike honey, comes out of the holes. Round, like a millstone, the cheeses weigh between 12 lb. and 25 lb.

PECORINO (Italian) – A hard cheese made from ewe's milk in Sardinia. It is a strong cheese with a piquant flavour and sometimes preferred to Parmesan in cheese dishes.

PETIT GRUYÈRE (Dutch) – This cheese originated in Holland, but is now produced in nearly every country, processed and packed in round boxes containing twelve or six portions. It is a soft, white cheese and does not resemble Gruyère at all.

PETIT SUISSE (French) – An unsalted cream cheese now made in most countries and sold in various forms, sometimes square, sometimes round. The original Petit Suisse is cylindrical and about 2 inches in diameter.

PONT L'ÉVÊQUE (French) – A semi-hard cheese ripened in cellars over a period of four months. It is small, 4 inches or so square, has a pale, straw-coloured paste and dark-brown chequered crust.

PORT SALUT (French) – A semi-hard cheese, round, 8 to 10 inches in diameter and 2 inches thick. The outer skin is orange, the cheese itself pale yellow. It is, supposedly, made in Trappist monasteries all over France, according to a secret formula, but of late has been advertised on television and sold in quarters wrapped in cellophane, which leads one to doubt its esoteric origin.

ROQUEFORT (French) – The most famous, with gorgonzola, of the blue-veined cheeses and the only ewe's milk cheese to attain world-wide popularity. Mouldy breadcrumbs mixed in the cheese play a great part in its unique taste, but so do the limestone caves in which it is matured. Round, 6 inches in diameter, 3 inches high.

STILTON (English) – A semi-hard blue-veined cheese and possibly the most famous of all English cheeses enjoying a 'high' reputation abroad. It takes a good nine months to ripen, and though port is often added, this is not really necessary and has caused some controversy among cheese gourmets. As tall as it is wide, it is drum-shaped and a foot across. The cheese is dug out from its centre like paté from a tureen.

SUFFOLK (English) – Even harder than Parmesan. There is a saying that 'hunger will break through stone walls and anything except Suffolk cheese'.

TOMME AU RAISIN (French) – A semi-hard cheese peppered outwardly with grape pips, giving it a strange raisin flavour and causing a certain amount of discomfort to the eater. Drum-shaped, it is small, about 4 inches in diameter.

WENSLEYDALE (English) – There are two types of Wensleydale, the first a blue-veined cheese not unlike Stilton but smaller, the second a flat white cheese which is eaten fresh. Both come from the Vale of Wensleydale in Yorkshire.

14

CONDIMENTS AND SPICES

CONDIMENTS and spices are synonymous with perfume. They add to, they enhance, they improve.

The Egyptians started it all, the Romans made it an art, and the practice of spicing foods and perfuming bodies gained popularity as civilization expanded.

It was early in the fifteenth century that things started going a bit wrong when the German Emperor insisted on having his girls rubbed with spices so that he could choose the one whose breath smelt most of tarragon, or coriander, depending on the time of day. But that was nothing to what happened later.

At Versailles, under Louis XIV, they went quite mad, reversing the German idea by perfuming all their food. Orris root and rosewater was freely sprinkled on meats, pastries and pies, walnuts were flavoured with musk, cream whipped up with ambergris and eggs bathed in scents.

This, however, might have been a late reaction to the fear of spices that was present under the Borgias, for one of the most respected persons in the Pope's household was the chef spicer. It was he who knew how to disguise the taste of a poison with the use of condiments.

Spices in the past had the reputation of being very

expensive, due to the fact that most came from far away places, but considering the modern travelling facilities, the work they do and the small amounts used, they can no longer be looked upon as extravagant.

The Romans thought them valuable, of course, and gladly exchanged a man for a bag of pepper.

ALLSPICE – From the West Indies. The dried, unripe berry of the Jamaican pepper. Also the name given to cultivated Nigella.

ANISEED – From the Middle East, mostly Egypt, but grows also in Spain, Switzerland and the South of France. A plant with small ovoid seeds. Used with sweets, in cakes and confectionery, but distilled makes the famous pernod. Sometimes added to flavour fish stews.

BASIL – Grown in this country, a common herb. The tips of this six inch high plant and the leaves are used in salads and soups when dried and rubbed to a powder.

BAY – Grows in this country, a bush of the laurel-tree family the leaves of which are highly perfumed by a sweet oil. The dried leaves should be used in moderation due to the fact that when cooked they not only give off a pleasant aroma, but, after a while, a slightly bitter taste as well.

BURNET – An aromatic meadow plant.

CAPERS – From Algeria, Turkey and the South of France, capers are the floral buds of the caper bush. Some are grown in England but they are not as round or as firm. Capers are pickled in vinegar before being used.

CARDAMOM – From India. The seed capsules of the cardamom plant are used whole or ground and are as hot as ginger. One of the ingredients used in making curry powder.

CHERVIL – Grows in this country. A parsley-type herb used fresh, and dried for various seasonings.

CHIVES – Grows in this country. A member of the onion family. The leaves, which are round, hollow and long, but very thin, are used for flavouring salads and certain dishes.

CINNAMON – From Ceylon. The bark of the cinnamon tree with a delicate sweet-hot taste and aroma. Sold in long strips of rolled bark, it is yellow in colour and powdered for use.

CLOVES – From East India and China. The dried flower buds of the clove-tree. Half an inch in length, black with four-sided stems, they do not look unlike a complicated nail and are, in fact, called *Clou* (nail) *de Girofle* in France.

CORIANDER – From Southern Europe and the Near East. The fruit, about the size of a small cherry, from a plant. The flowers give off an unpleasant smell, but the fruit is bitter-sweet and used for flavouring spirits as well as seasoning a variety of foods.

CUMIN – From the Near and Far East. The long yellow seeds of the cumin plant are distinguishable by their hairy growth. Used in bread, Munster cheese and liqueurs, their taste is pleasantly acrid.

FENNEL – Grown in this country, but originally an Italian plant. Tall, flowering, it has a bean-like bulbous growth at the bottom of each leaf stem, which is cooked like celery, but this and the leaf itself is also used to flavour a variety of dishes.

GINGER – From China and India, the East and West Indies. A root which, when cut, is either white, grey or yellow. Strong and hot, apt to make one sneeze. Used grated, as a flavouring agent, with a variety of foods and in jam and sweets.

JUNIPER – Grows in this country, wild. Juniper berries are used as a flavouring agent for many meat dishes and also in the distillation of gin.

MACE – From East India. The dried shell of the nutmeg and slightly stronger in flavour. Mainly used in pickling and brines, but also flavours a variety of dishes.

MARJORAM – Grows in this country. An aromatic herb used for flavouring when dried and rubbed.

MINT – Grows in this country. There are many varieties of this plant, one of which is the peppermint, a far more pungent type than the one normally grown in back gardens, used for the making of Crème de Menthe and cordials. Fresh mint, chopped and bathed in vinegar with sugar is used as a sauce with lamb. Rubbed dried mint is a substitute.

MUSTARD – Grows in Northern Europe and America. The black and white seeds are ground to a powder and mixed with different liquids (verjuice or wine) to obtain various mustards. Turmeric is added to a blend of black and white seeds to make the strong English mustard – invented in 1720.

NASTURTIUM – Grown in this country. An edible plant, the flowers and leaves tasting like water-cress. The flowers are sometimes used in salads with the leaves; the buds, when young, are pickled like capers.

NIGELLA – From Egypt. The seeds of this flowering plant vary in strength, but some are used instead of pepper.

NUTMEG – From India and the East Indies. The nut of the

nutmeg tree – oval, greyish brown – it is used, grated, in a large number of preparations.

PAPRIKA – Originated in Turkey, now grows in the warmer parts of Europe and America. Paprika is the fine red powder made from ground, dried, black pimento seeds – mainly in Hungary.

PARSLEY – Grows in this country. A dark, bright-green, curly-leafed plant which is used extensively in the kitchen as a garnish to cold dishes, chopped in salads or mixed with butter for hot dishes and as the 'bit of greenery' on most cold meat and fish presentations.

PEPPER – Not to be confused with pimento, which bears the same name in England. Grows in the tropics of Asia and America. Pepper is the berry of a vine-like plant (the pepper plant), which is picked before it is ripe, and ground. Once ground, pepper loses much of its flavour; it is therefore mostly used in pepper mills to get all the 'instant' aroma. There are two varieties, black and white, on the market. The latter is the same as the former only with the skin and fleshy part of the berry removed before it is dried.

PURSLANE – Grows in this country. A weed, the leaves of which are preserved in vinegar and used as condiment. Fresh, it is sometimes eaten as a salad or cooked as a vegetable.

ROSEMARY – Grows in this country. A flowering shrub, the leaves and stems of which are used for flavouring when dried and rubbed.

SAFFRON – Cultivated specially in France and Spain, saffron is the dried stamens of the saffron crocus, which was brought to Europe from the East by the Arabs. The dried stamens, which are thin, dark brick-red filaments streaked with white, look like pipe-tobacco and give off a bright yellow hue when in contact with liquids. The aroma, valued in cooking, is quite unique.

SAGE – Grows in this country. An evergreen shrub which stands some three feet high. The aromatic leaves are used extensively, specially in this country, for flavouring and stuffings. The best sage comes from Provence.

SAVORY – Grows in this country. An aromatic herb not unlike thyme.

TARRAGON – Grows in this country. An aromatic herb used in flavouring salads and sauces.

THYME – Grows in this country. A refreshing, aromatic herb with a pleasant, pungent smell used in the flavouring of soups, sauces and salads.

TURMERIC – From India. A powder made from the dried and ground stem of the turmeric plant. Similar in flavour to ginger, it is, however, more delicate. Like saffron, gives off a bright yellow hue.

TURTLE HERBS – Basil, bay leaves, marjoram and thyme mixed together and used in soups and sauces.

VANILLA – From Mexico, also cultivated in other tropical countries. Vanilla is a climbing plant, the pods of which are gathered when they are not quite ripe, and dried in enclosed containers. This airtight condition develops their aroma. Vanilla pods vary in size but grow to a length of eight inches. It is used as a flavouring agent in its dry-stick form, powdered or as an extract, usually for the sweeter dishes.

VERJUICE – The juice of unripe grapes quite often used in sauces and other preparations.

WORMWOOD – An alpine herb found mostly in Switzerland.

15

WINES, SPIRITS AND LIQUEURS

THERE is more rubbish talked about wine and wine-tasting than anything else. It is the perfect subject for the snob, the one-up man, the bore and, because the true experts are patient and polite people who prefer drinking wine to talking about it, only the views of the amateur are expressed and they become more and more banal as time goes on.

To sample a few wines with a *sommelier* in the cellars of a restaurant is one thing, to listen to the conversation of wine-men during a 'wine-tasting' is another.

'Boisterous would you say?'

'Crisp.'

'Crisp? Perhaps. An unmistakable tang of flintstone.'

'I'd call it flippant.'

'It is a bit naughty, one must admit.'

'Playful, just playful.'

Or, to quote James Thurber, 'It's a naïve domestic Burgundy without any breeding, but I think you'll be amused by its presumption.'

On more than one occasion I have decanted a rather lousy Algerian into a Lynch-Bages bottle and watched my guests go into raptures over its 'bouquet' – I am not a good host. Nor am I impressed by anyone who spends more than five seconds tasting a wine in a restaurant. It should be done discreetly, a quick sniff to smell if the wine is corked – it does happen – and a quick taste to test the temperature which is important. If too warm, a discreet whisper to the waiter who should quietly deal with the matter, if too cold a word to your guests about it, advising them to warm the wine glass in the palm of their hand. A red wine can never be warmed as a white wine can be cooled.

To follow the advice of a typical pamphlet found on the counter of a wine merchant is, I think, heading for ridicule. I quote:

The art of tasting wine is the performance of a sacred rite, which deserves to be carried out with the most grave and serious attention.

The sense of taste should be neutralized and the palate cleared with a little bread or cheese. Take neither water, tobacco nor sweets.

Fill the glass only half full so that the fragrance of the wine will gather in the vacant upper space.

Inhale its fragrance, revolving the glass gently in the hand to obtain the aroma to the fullest extent.

Taste it in small sips, savouring it so as to appreciate fully its sweetness, or dryness, its body.

Finally, analyse your reactions and try to describe them, using the vocabulary of the connoisseur. Thus you will come to be acknowledged and respected as an accomplished wine-taster. And you can add to your reputation by relating anecdotes of the wines of France.

A sure short cut to becoming the comedian of the evening.

As far as I am concerned there are only two types of wine, those I like, those I don't like, and it is simply a matter of trial and error to find out which wines you prefer.

It is not necessary for anyone to love champagne, nor is it essential to turn one's nose up at a *vin ordinaire*, nor for that matter will you be admired for praising to the heights a *vin ordinaire* and telling everyone you can't bear champagne. The danger with wine in England is that, for certain people, it has a prestige value. This is a pity. You should drink it, enjoy it and shut up.

But what is wine? In short, the process of wine-making is as follows. The grapes are collected from the vines and the juice is pressed out. The juice is then allowed to ferment (a bacteriological process in which living micro-organisms increase and multiply with the help of oxygen from the air). The first fermentation, therefore, takes place in open vats. The young wine is then poured into covered vats for the second fermentation, during which the thick wine clears by throwing a deposit.

After a few months, the clearer wine is separated from the deposit and poured into clean casks where it is refined further by the addition of white of egg or gelatine which, mixing with the tannin in the wine, forms a further deposit.

This wine is left to mature for a period of two to four years and then it is put into bottles where it continues to mature, in certain cases.

Needless to say, variations on this very basic process are employed according to the character of the wine to be produced.

The greatest wine-producing country in the world is

France, making some fifteen hundred million gallons a year. Italy produces just over half that amount and Spain a half of Italy's production. Though many countries make wine, the very best comes from France and Germany, the latter getting its name for quality not quantity. In order of production importance the top twenty are as follows: France, Italy, Spain, Algeria, Portugal, Argentina, Greece, U.S.A., Rumania, Hungary, Chile, Yugoslavia, South Africa, Germany, Russia, Australia, Morocco, Brazil, Uruguay and Tunisia.

The principal wines of France come from the Alsace, Beaujolais, Bordeaux, Burgundy, Champagne, Côtes du Rhône and Loire areas. Germany is famous for its Hocks and Moselles.

If you wish to become an expert on wine there are literally countless books on the subject, wine clubs, wine magazines, apart from all the merchants and shippers who can load you with tons of literature on their products. You can learn about wine-making, bottling, labelling, vintages, temperatures, countries of origin, types of glasses, types of bottles, types of vine – it can be a lifetime hobby.

Briefly, for it would take a whole book to discuss wine, if you arm yourself with a vintage chart – easily obtainable from most wine merchants – you can learn the best years for the best wines and, if you know you can rely on a good merchant, you cannot make too many mistakes.

The top-class wines are always a good bet when entertaining important guests, and these are as follows:

From ALSACE, an area in the north-east of France, between the Vosges Mountains and the Rhine – Riesling, Sylvaner, Traminer or Geurztraminer. The wine is sold almost always by the name of the grape so there are no vineyard names to remember.

BEAUJOLAIS, an area just to the north of Lyons, produces, together with vineyards in the Mâcon district, the red Fleuris, Thorins, Moulin à Vent and Morgon, the white Pouilly and Fuissé. Beaujolais wines do not improve with age.

CLARET is the traditional English name for the red wines of BORDEAUX. There is no such thing as a white claret though, of course, there is a white Bordeaux, which is all very confusing and of no value to anyone.

The variety of names on wine labels is also confusing, but for a reason – that of preserving the quality of the wines. The strict laws of 'Appellation d'origine contrôleé' not only limit certain wines to certain plots, but also specifiy the vines that should be planted, the methods of pruning and of cultivation, and the quality of the grapes.

On a label there is therefore the name of the area (Bordeaux), the name of the region in that area (Médoc), the name of a commune within that region (St Estèphe) and the name of a château in that commune. Also the date the wine was bottled and the name of the shipper.

The Bordeaux area is around the Gironde, south-west France, and the finest red wines are those of the Médoc, Graves, St Emilion and Pomerol regions. The finest whites from Sauternes.

BURGUNDY covers an area around Dijon, east of Switzerland, north of Lyons. The best red and white wines come from the Côte d'Or region, the most renowned white – Chablis.

CHAMPAGNE lies to the north-east of Burgundy. The

famous wines from this area differ from the others mainly because they are bottled before fermentation begins – producing the all-important bubbles – and because the wines of different vineyards are blended to make one wine. When the wines of different vineyards and different years are blended then the champagne is labelled 'Non-vintage'.

Also, unlike other wines, Champagne is known under the name of the shipper, who maintains a standard for his reputation's sake. Among the leading brands, the best known are: Bollinger, Heidsieck, Irroy, Krug, Lanson, Moet & Chandon, Mumm, Pommery, Taittinger and Veuve Clicquot.

THE CÔTES DU RHÔNE wines come from the Rhône valley below Lyons. The best are Côte Rôtie, Châteauneuf du Pape and Hermitage.

The LOIRE area produces sweeter wines than most, the white Vin d'Anjou and Vin de Touraine. The finest Anjou are Château de l'Aiglerie, Château de Parnay. In Touraine, farther up the river, the well-known white wines are Vouvray, Montlouis and Rochecorbon. The red wines of Bourgueil are reputed the best of their colour on the Loire.

When speaking of German wines, the names of HOCK and MOSELLE come to mind. These again are names of areas, though the former originates from the town of Hochheim, which is nowhere near the vineyards of Rheingau, Rheinhesse, and Palatinate, which produce the wines.

Moselles come from the German part of the valley of the river Moselle (or Mosel) which flows into the Rhine at Coblenz.

A quick-glance recognition of Hocks and Moselles can

be done by looking at the colour of the bottles. Hocks are bottled in reddish glass, Moselles in blueish-green.

ABSINTHE – A liqueur made by the distillation of wormwood leaves, fennel, anise and other aromatic herbs and plants. Invented by a certain Doctor Ordinaire, the recipe was bought at the end of the eighteenth century by Monsieur Pernod whose name has been associated with the drink ever since.

ADVOCAAT – A Dutch liqueur made of egg-yolks and brandy.

AQUAVIT-AKVAVIT – A Scandinavian spirit distilled from potatoes or grain, flavoured with caraway seeds.

AMONTILLADO – A type of medium sherry which should be served before meals, slightly chilled.

AMOROSO – A rich type of sherry, much darker and sweeter than amontillado. Should be served at the beginning or the very end of a meal.

ANISETTE – A French liqueur made with aniseed.

APRICOT BRANDY – A Hungarian liqueur distilled from fresh apricots and the crushed kernels of the stones.

ARMAGNAC – Brandy distilled from the wines of the Gers Department in south-west France, north of the Pyrénées, west of Toulouse. A good armagnac is better than an average cognac, but not better than a good cognac.

ARRACK – An Indian spirit distilled from rice.

BACARDI – A Cuban rum.

BENEDICTINE – A French liqueur from Fécamp in Normandy, reputed to be the oldest liqueur, invented and still made by Benedictine monks.

BOURBON – An American whisky distilled from fermented maize and other grains.

BRANDY – A spirit distilled from wine – or fermented grape juice, which is wine. It can be distilled wherever wine is available.

CALVADOS – A spirit distilled from cider made with apples from Calvados orchards, north-west France. It is clear, of very high strength and kept in wood.

CHARTREUSE – A French liqueur, which originated in the Grande Chartreuse Monastery near Grenoble. Invented by Carthusian monks in 1607 it was made only by them till the turn of this century. Now it is manufactured in large quantities. There are two types of Chartreuse, green and yellow. The green is the stronger of the two.

COGNAC – Brandy distilled in the Cognac district, just inland in the centre of the west coast of France, north of Bordeaux. The vineyards that produce the special wines for distilling are those of Borderies, Grande and Petite Champagne. No other brandy can be called Cognac, for it has a strict geographical meaning. Grande Champagne, Fine Champagne and Petite Champagne also correspond to very distinct areas. These names have nothing whatsoever to do with the sparkling wine. Cognac is sold under various labels which guarantee its age, though not its quality. One Star not less than three years old. Two Stars not less than four years old. Three Stars not less than five years old. V.S.O. (Very Special Old) from 12 to 17 years old. V.S.O.P. (Very Special Old Pale) from 18 to 25 years old. V.V.S.O.P. (Very V.S.O.P.) from 25 years old.

COINTREAU – A French curaçao made with oranges and

clear in colour. Its strength varies, depending on the country it is sold in.

CRÈME DE – ANANAS, BANANES, CASSIS, FRAISES, FRAMBOISES, MENTHE, MOKA, NOYAU, VANILLE, VIOLETTE, etc. . . . French liqueurs with flavours denoted by the name. Usually extremely sweet.

CURAÇAO – A Dutch liqueur originally made with green Curaçao oranges, gin and brandy. Now made in other countries under other names. E.g., Cointreau.

DRAMBUIE – A Scottish liqueur made with Scotch whisky and honey.

EAU DE VIE – The French for drinkable spirit. If distilled from cider, then Eau de Vie de Cidre. From various fruits, then Eau de Vie de Fruits.

GENTIANE – A Swiss liqueur made from the ground roots of the gentian, a herbaceous plant found in the mountains.

GIN – A spirit distilled from grain and flavoured with juniper berries. The English and Dutch gins are the most famous.

GRAND MARNIER – A French brand name for a curaçao sold under two labels, Cordon Rouge and Cordon Jaune. The latter is the weaker and sweeter of the two.

GRAPPA – An Italian spirit distilled from the pips, skins and stalks of grapes left over after the grapes have been pressed for wine.

KIRSCH – A German spirit distilled from the fermented juices of black cherries found in the Black Forest. It is also distilled in Switzerland and Alsace. Clear in colour.

KÜMMEL – A Dutch liqueur made with a spirit distilled from potatoes or grain and flavoured with caraway seeds and cumin.

MADEIRA – A fortified wine made with special grapes grown on the island of Madeira. Malmsey Madeira is very sweet, Bual Madeira less so, but rich; Special Madeira is dry.

MARSALA – An Italian dessert wine made with grapes from Sicily.

MEAD – An old English beverage made with fermented, honeyed water, flavoured with a variety of strong aromatic herbs.

MIRABELLE – A French spirit distilled from Mirabelles, small golden plums.

PRUNELLE – A French liqueur made from sloes.

MARC – Like Grappa, a spirit distilled from the remains of grapes crushed for wine. Also made with the remains of apples crushed for making cider.

RUM – A spirit distilled from molasses or fermented juice of the sugar cane.

RYE WHISKY – A spirit distilled from a fermented mash of rye grain.

SAKÉ – A Japanese beverage made from the fermented brew of grains and rice.

SLOE GIN – A liqueur made with gin and flavoured with sloes (blackthorn berries). Sticky and sweet if drunk too soon. After ten years it is a clean and mellow drink.

VAN DER HUM – A South African liqueur made with Cape brandy and tangerines.

VODKA – A Russian spirit, distilled from fermented wheat.

WHISKY – A spirit distilled from barley, rye and other cereals, malted before being allowed to ferment.

16

THE MENU

Though the word 'menu' originates from the Latin 'minutus' – meaning small – and the Romans were the first to cultivate, prepare and eat many of the delicacies we enjoy today, as well as considering banqueting an art and spreading their culinary wisdom all over Europe, they did not invent the menu. This they left to the Duke of Brunswick, who, as late as 1541, was the first to draw up a list of all the foods his chef could prepare, so that his guests could reserve their appetites for their favourite dishes.

This obviously intelligent idea became fashionable immediately, and has been with us ever since, now serving two useful purposes, that of listing what is available and giving the price.

The French called the list 'menu' because its function is to help whittle down to a few dishes the very great number suggested.

A menu is compiled by the chef, who decides what he can offer, depending on his capabilities and the foods that are in season, also the type of people for whom he is catering.

The reason why menus are written mostly in French is that the majority of traditional dishes originated in France, though when dishes come from other countries they are usually listed in their native language. For example, the Italian Spaghetti Bolognese or Saltimbocca alla Romana are not written in French, nor are Yorkshire Pudding, Welsh Rarebit or Irish Stew.

There are two types of menu – *à la carte* and *table d'hôte*. The *à la carte* (on the card) menu is a list of everything the chef thinks he can conceivably offer and, in the best restaurants, an *à la carte* menu lists every type of dish that is in season. More often than not the various dishes come under their appropriate headings: Appetizers, Soups, Eggs, Fish, Pastas, Entrées, Assorted Cold Meats, Grills, Vegetables, Sweets, Cheeses, Savouries.

While, when dining *à la carte*, you have the advantage of eating whatever you wish, you must be ready to wait for the dish of your choice, as it will be cooked specially for you and no one else. This takes time.

For instance, you must expect to wait at least ten minutes for specially prepared soups, egg dishes, omelettes, potatoes. Fifteen minutes for liver or veal, steaks, fish, lamb chops; twenty-five minutes for roast chicken and soufflés, and the best part of forty minutes for anything like a chicken *en cocotte*.

The *table d'hôte* (table of the host) originated when hurried travellers found it convenient to sit down at mine host's table to share his food already prepared, consuming several courses for a fixed price.

The *table d'hôte* has changed little and definite dishes are still offered for a certain price.

Though most people today only eat four or five courses, the full traditional menu is composed of twelve.

MENU

Hors d'Oeuvre
Potage—Poisson—Entrée
Relevé
Sorbet
Rôti—Légumes
Entremets—Savoury
Coffee and Liqueurs

1. *Hors d'œuvre*, meaning outside (hors) the masterpiece (œuvre) – the meal, consists of various preparations designed to whet the appetite. Hors d'œuvre include a large number of small dishes, sardines, salami, olives, salads, etc., but also *foie gras*, caviare, oysters, smoked salmon, melon, grapefruit, etc.

2. *Potage* (Soup). – Two soups are usually suggested, a consommé (clear) or a crème (thick). It is not usual for people to have both.

3. *Poisson* (Fish) – This is self-explanatory, but depends on the fish in season.

4. *Entrée* – This heading is misleading, for the translation means 'entry', suggesting the beginning, when it is not, though it is the first meat course. Entrées are complete dishes in themselves, e.g.: *Jambon d'York aux Épinards en Feuilles, Foie de Veau Sauté au Bacon, Rumpsteak Grillé Continentale.*

5. *Relevé* (or Remove) – This is the main meat course and may consist of lamb, baron of beef, venison, etc.

6. *Sorbet* – This is a rest between courses, and counteracts the effects of the dishes already served. A sorbet is a water ice which should be flavoured with champagne, served in tall, small glasses.

7. *Rôti* (Roast). – This course signifies poultry or winged game.

8. *Légume* (Vegetable) – A special dish of vegetables, artichokes or asparagus perhaps.

9. *Entremets* (Desserts) – The word *entremets* like *entrée* is misleading, for, translated, means 'between courses'. In France it makes a little more sense as cheeses are served before the dessert, and therefore entremets come between

the cheese and the savoury, but in England cheeses are usually served after the sweets. Entremets may be hot or cold desserts.

   10. *Savoury* – Various tit-bits on toast or cheese.

   11. *Desserts* – Fresh fruits in season.

   12. *Coffee and Liqueurs.*

Due to quick-frozen processes, a great number of foods are now available all the year round, but for those who prefer 'fresh' edibles when they are *really* fresh, the following list may help. These foods are plentiful and in their prime in England during the months shown:

Apricots	May to August.
Artichokes	December to June.
Asparagus	January to September.
Barbel	July to March.
Bass	May to September.
Brill	August to March.
Broad Beans	June to August.
Broccoli	October to April.
Brussels Sprouts	October to March.
Carp	August to February.
Carrots (new)	May to June.
Cauliflowers	March to November.
Celeriac	October to March.
Celery	August to March.
Cherries	May to August.
Chestnuts	November to February.
Cod's Roe	February to April.
Corn on the Cob	August to October.

Cranberries	November to February.
Crawfish (*Langousté*)	June to September.
Crayfish (*Écrevisse*)	July to February.
Cucumbers	April to August.
Currants, all kinds	May to September.
Damsons	August to October.
Eels	September to May.
Endives	November to March.
Figs	August to October.
Flageolets	July to September.
Flounders	August to April.
French Beans	June to October.
Geese	September to February.
Gooseberries	April to July.
Greengages	June to September.
Hares	August to March.
Herrings	August to February.
Jerusalem Artichokes	October to February.
Lobsters	June to September.
Mackerel	April to October.
Mulberries	August to September.
Mullets	April to November.
Mussels	September to April.
Nectarines	July to October.
Parsnips	October to April.
Peaches	May to October.
Pears	August to December.
Peas	July to October.
Perch	July to March.
Plaice	May to January.
Plover's Eggs	April to May.

Plums	July to October.
Prawns	May to October.
Quinces	October to February.
Raspberries	June to September.
Rhubarb	December to July.
Salmon	11 February to September.
Salsiby	October to March.
Scollops	September to May.
Seakale	December to May.
Shrimps	April to September.
Skate	September to May.
Sole	July to March.
Sprats	November to March.
Strawberries	April to September.
Sturgeon	August to March.
Tangerines	November to June.
Tench	July to February.
Trout	1 April to October.
Turkey	October to February.
Venison	July to March.
Whitebait	February to September.
Whiting	August to February.

Having digested all these facts it may be that you will wish to put theory into practice and not only dine out with friends in various restaurants, but possibly elaborate on the traditions as some people found it amusing to do in the past.

Certain eccentric characters with rare imaginations and a flair for 'living it up' have given some splendid banquets and, though such occasions are less frequent, it would be nice if someone tried to compete with, for instance, the man who broke the bank at Monte Carlo. Having won on 'rouge' he celebrated his luck by giving a dinner for thirty-six of his intimate friends on a large roulette table and everything was red. The Press, in fact, referred to it as the Red Dinner at the Savoy. Everything from the carpet to the ceiling in the saloon was red. The waiters wore red costumes; their shirts, ties and gloves were red. There were red flowers everywhere, the electric lights were red. The dinner was composed of Prawns, *Queues de Langouste en Aspic, Crème Portugaise, Saumon à la Nantua, Mousse au Jambon, Filet de Bœuf aux Tomates farcies, Choux Rouges braisés, Poularde à la Cardinale, Canard Sauvage au Sang, Salade de Betterave, Mousse aux Fraises*, all of which were red, and by the time it had all been paid for it was rumoured that his bank account was in a similar hue.

In Leicester, in 1910, a dinner was eaten on one of the four dials of the clock which was eventually erected on the Royal Liver Insurance building in Liverpool. The dial, some twenty-five feet across, was used as the table and seated thirty-eight guests around it – members of the staff of the clock's manufacturers.

In 1914 a dinner was given by Hendon airmen for two colleagues who were the first to fly upside down and loop-the-loop. The banquet was an 'upside down' banquet, with the whole dinner served in reverse, starting with coffee and liqueurs and ending with hors d'œuvre. It was eaten off tables turned upside down set out in the shape of a loop.

There was a dinner given in honour of Arctic explorers, when the banqueting room was transformed to represent the North Pole, with an iceberg in the centre of the table and all the waiters dressed as Eskimos.

The president of a famous golf club also gave a dinner on a table which represented a miniature golf course, with trees and bunkers and lakes and a green.

And in America there was the craze for 'jungle' dinners. One, given by an amateur lion-tamer in a large cage, was eaten while four fully grown lions, who were treated with the same dainties as the guests, roamed about at will. Though the majority of the guests were brave, on one or two occasions some were seen to leap up and grow pale as a monarch of the forest playfully nuzzled a leg or a foot.

A wealthy Chicago lady, noted for her daring feats as an expert mountain climber, once gave a banquet on the roof of her house. There was nothing very exceptional about the food, but the guests had to come dressed in their mountain gear, with all their equipment, and climb up the face of the house to eat it.

An interesting dinner recorded recently was given by a rich amateur horticulturist whose reputation as a wit and gourmet rivalled that of his green fingers.

When visited one day by a boring relative, who lavished an excess of compliments on his blooms, he invited the man to join him for the evening meal and led him into a sumptuous dining-hall where a table was ready laid promising a feast to end all feasts.

The dinner, served by two lackeys, started with a small carnation served on a gold plate, which the host gently picked up and sniffed.

The second course was a bunch of pansies, which the host gently picked up and sniffed, and the third course a beautiful magnolia floating on water, served in a cut-crystal bowl. The fourth course was a mass of pom-pom dahlias, which did not smell particularly sweet, this was followed by a spray of tiger lilies and the meal ended with the delicate intake of the scent of violets.

A beautifully composed menu, though not satisfying to the hungry relative, who left surprisingly early and was never seen again.

A GLOSSARY OF FRENCH MENU TERMS

THE following glossary includes the majority of names currently given to dishes, garnishes, sauces, soups and, *separately*, potato preparations. Also terms referring to them.

It should be borne in mind that every chef has his own special dishes which he may dedicate to himself, his wife, his mistress or favourite horse, sometimes unintentionally giving the same name to two completely different recipes, or a new name to an established recipe.

Abatis – Giblets.
Abats – Offal.
Africaine (*à l' Africaine*) – A garnish of rare purple potatoes cut down to marble size, cooked in butter, and small braised marrows, served with saffron-flavoured rice.
Agneau – Lamb.
Ail – Garlic.
Aileron – Pinion or poultry wing.
Aioli – A thick, smooth, garlic mayonnaise.
Albigeoise – Large or small cuts of meat garnished with chopped ham, potato croquettes and small tomatoes stuffed with mushrooms, onions, breadcrumbs, garlic and parsley.
Alboni – A white wine sauce served with venison.
Albuféra – Poached chicken stuffed with a *salpicon* of *foie*

gras, truffles and rice, garnished with cocks' kidneys, mushrooms, calve's tongue, and tartlets of small ball-shaped truffles.

Algérienne (à l'Algérienne) – A dish garnished with small tomatoes braised in oil and sweet potatoes cooked in butter.

Allemande – A thick sauce made with meat, poultry or fish stock, used as a foundation to many other sauces.

Allumettes – Matchsticks of puff pastry cooked in the oven with different flavoured garnishes. Also potatoes finely cut like matchsticks.

Alose – Shad – a slightly larger fish than the herring that spawns in fresh water in the spring.

Alouette – Lark.

Aloyau – Sirloin.

Alsacienne – Large cuts of meat, goose, duck and other poultry garnished with Strasbourg sausage, braised sauerkraut and boiled potatoes.

Amande – Almond.

Ambassadrice – Poultry and small cuts of meat garnished with sautéed chicken livers, shredded truffles, sautéed mushrooms, cocks' combs and cocks' kidneys. Madeira sauce.

Américaine (à l'Américaine) – A dish prepared with peeled and pressed tomatoes cooked in oil or butter and spiced chopped onions, shallots, garlic, parsley, chervil and tarragon with added white wine or brandy.

Ananas – Pineapple.

Anchois – Anchovy.

Ancienne (à l'ancienne) – A term applied to blanquettes and fricassées of veal and chicken.

Andalouse (à l'Andalouse) – Dishes served with tomatoes, sweet pimentos, aubergines, rice pilaf and chipolata sausages.

Andouille – A large cooked sausage served as cold slices, composed of highly seasoned pigs' intestines and strips of chitterlings.

Andouillettes – Chitterlings.

Anglaise (à l'Anglaise) – Ingredients coated in a mixture composed of eggs, oil, salt, and pepper, breadcrumbed then deep fried. *Or* mutton, chicken or vegetables boiled in water or in a white stock. *Or* fish grilled and served with melted butter.

Anis Vert – Aniseed.

Anversoise (à l'Anversoise) – Poached leg of lamb garnished with artichoke hearts, stuffed with hop shoots in cream, and served with small, round fried potatoes.

Archiduc (à l'Archiduc) – Dishes seasoned with paprika and blended with cream.

Ardenaise (à l'Ardenaise) – Small birds cooked in a casserole with juniper berries.

Ariégoise (à l'Ariégoise) – Dishes garnished with pickled pork, green cabbage and red beans.

Arlésienne (à l'Arlésienne) – There are three different garnishes which come under this name, all include tomatoes:

1. Small tomatoes stuffed with rice pilaf, large olives stuffed with chicken stuffing, anchovy butter, and new potatoes.

2. Sautéed tomatoes, fried onion rings, and fried aubergines.

3. Whole peeled stewed tomatoes with fried chicory hearts.

Armoricaine (*à l'Armoricaine*) – This is a corruption of *à l'Américaine*. See *Américaine*.

Artagnan (*à l'Artagnan*) – Meat and poultry garnished with *cèpes*, stuffed tomatoes and potato croquettes.

Artichaut – Artichoke.

Asperge – Asparagus.

Aspic – Fillets or slices of meat, poultry, game, fish, vegetables or fruit presented in jelly moulds of varying flavours.

Assiette Anglaise – A variety of cold meats and *charcuterie* served with gherkins, watercress and chopped jelly.

Attereaux – Skewered preparations, usually hors d'œuvre, coated with a sauce, rolled in breadcrumbs, and deep fried.

Aubergine – Egg plant.

Aurore (*à l'Aurore*) – Sweetbreads, eggs or poultry served with a thick tomato sauce.

Autrichienne (*à l'Autrichienne*) – Dishes seasoned with paprika, lightly fried onions and sour cream.

Auvergnat – Dishes usually served with chestnuts.

Avoine – Oats.

*

Baba – A cake of leavened dough mixed with raisins and steeped in rum or kirsch.

Ballotine – Meat, fowl, game, poultry or fish, boned, stuffed and rolled into a cylindrical shape.

Banquière (*à la Banquière*) – A garnish for *vol-au-vents*, chicken, sweetbreads, composed of mushrooms, slivers of truffle, *quenelles* laced with a madeira sauce.

Bar – Bass – the fish.

Barbeau – Barbel.

Barbue – Brill.

Barigoule (*à la Barigoule*) – Usually refers to stuffed artichokes – the stuffing being left to the chef.

Basquaise (*à la Basquaise*)– Large cuts of meat garnished with fried *cèpes*, potatoes and Bayonne ham.

Bâtons – Various dessert preparations presented in the shape of sticks. Also *Bâtonnets*.

Bavarois – Bavarian cream – a custard whisked with gelatine, topped with fresh whipped cream.

Bavaroise – A hot evening drink of strong tea to which is added a yolk of egg, sugar, sugar syrup, boiled milk, rum, kirsch, maraschino, or other liqueurs.

Béarnaise – A sauce made of shallots, tarragon, chervil, thyme, bay leaves, vinegar, white wine, yolk of egg, butter, Cayenne pepper, salt, pepper and lemon juice. Usually served with meats.

Beatrix – Small cuts of meat garnished with braised artichokes, morels sautéed in butter, carrots and new potatoes.

Beauharnais (*à la Beauharnais*) – A garnish of small artichokes with Béarnaise sauce and purée of tarragon, served with little potato balls for small cuts of meat – specially tournedos.

Beauvilliers – Large cuts of meat, braised, garnished with small spinach-filled pancakes, tomatoes stuffed with cooked brain purée, and sautéed salsify slices.

Bécasse – Woodcock.

Bécassine – Snipe.

Béchamel – A white sauce made with milk, white roux, butter, flour, onion, thyme, bay leaves and grated nutmeg.

Beignets – Fritters.

Beluga – Caviare – from the largest of the sturgeon species called Beluga. Large grain.

Bénédictine (*à la Bénédictine*) – A garnish for eggs and poached fish composed of a white paste of salt cod cooked in oil and crushed garlic.

Bercy – A butter sauce composed of beef bone marrow, white wine, shallots, parsley and lemon juice. Served with grilled meats and fish.

Berrichonne (*à la Berrichonne*) – Mutton or other large cuts of meat garnished with braised cabbage, bacon, onion and chestnuts.

Betterave – Beetroot.

Beurre Noire – Butter browned with vinegar in the pan where the food to be garnished has been cooked.

Beurre Noisette – Melted butter removed from the fire when it has just started foaming. It has a slightly nutty taste and is hazel in colour.

Biarrotte (*à la Biarrotte*) – Small cuts of meat garnished with grilled *cèpes* and *duchesse* potatoes.

Bigarade – A rich orange sauce, served with duck.

Bischof (Bishop mulled wine) – Red wine heated and spiced with cinnamon, cloves, lemon and orange peel and aniseed.

Biscottes – Rusks.

Bisque – A thick soup or purée made with crayfish or other shellfish.

Blanquette – A white ragout of lamb or veal or chicken made with yolks of egg and cream and garnished with small onions and mushrooms.

Blé – Wheat.

Bleu (*au bleu*) – A method of cooking fresh-water fish by plunging it into boiling water seasoned with vinegar and salt and spiced with bay leaves and thyme.

Bœuf – Beef.

Bombe – Ice cream.

Bonne Femme (*à la Bonne Femme*) – Dishes, usually sole, cooked in the oven with butter and mushrooms.

Bonnefoy – A white wine sauce with finely chopped shallots, served with grills.

Bordelaise (*à la Bordelaise*) – Meat dishes served with a *demi-glace* sauce to which is added red wine, shallots, thyme, bay leaf, sometimes served with *cèpes* or artichokes.

Bortsch – A Russian or Polish broth made with beetroot and other vegetables, fish, duck, or ham, garnished with ravioli and sour cream.

Bouchée à la Reine – A small *vol-au-vent* for one person.

Bouchées – Empty puff pastry patties filled with various preparations, savoury or sweet.

Boudin (Black pudding) – A large sausage made with cooked pig's blood.

Bouillabaisse – A Mediterranean fish dish originating from Marseille made with local fish which are cooked in white wine, with tomatoes, garlic, saffron, onions, cloves, fennel, parsley, thyme, bay leaf, orange peel. See also Chapter 9.

Bouillon – Broth.

Boule de Neige – Sponge cake or ice cream shaped like snowballs, over which a fresh whipped cream is poured.

Bouquet Garni – A bundle of aromatic herbs used to flavour stews, soups, and sauces made up of parsley, thyme, bay leaf, basil, celery, chervil, tarragon, savory, burnet, rosemary.

Bouquetière (à la Bouquetière) – A garnish for meat dishes consisting of artichoke hearts filled with chopped carrots and turnips, asparagus tips, buttered French beans, cauliflower served with Hollandaise sauce and either sautéed or new potatoes. This dish is usually carefully presented, the various vegetables being neatly arranged around the edge of the main dish in little 'bouquets'.

Bourgeoise (à la Bourgeoise or *à la Mode Bourgeoise)* – Braised meats garnished with carrots, onions and lean bacon.

Bourguignonne – (1) A method of preparing braised meat, poultry, fish and eggs, using a red wine sauce, mushrooms and onions. (2) *Bœuf Bourguignonne* – Cubes of raw steak plunged into boiling oil by guests at the table – similar to the *fondue* ritual. Also *Escargots à la Bourguignonne*, snails garnished with garlic butter and breadcrumbs.

Brabançonne (à la Brabançonne) – Large pieces of meat garnished with endives, potato croquettes or hop shoots cooked in butter or cream.

Brandade – A paste of pounded salt cod and garlic.

Bretonne (à la Bretonne) – Dishes served with cooked white beans and Bretonne sauce which consists of a *velouté* sauce thickened with finely shredded celery, leeks and carrots.

Brillat Savarin – Large or small cuts of meat garnished with *duchesse* potatoes filled with *foie gras* and truffles, served with asparagus and a white Malaga wine sauce.

Brioche – A cake in the shape of a ball with a smaller round head on it, made of yeast dough.

Brochet – Pike.

Brochette – A skewer on which preparations are threaded before grilling or frying. Similar to, but not to be confused with, *Attereaux*.

Brouiller – To scramble. *Œufs brouillés* is scrambled eggs.

Brunoise – Carrots, celery, leeks, onions, and turnips cooked in butter.

Bruxelloise – Large or small cuts of meat garnished with brussels sprouts and *fondantes* potatoes.

*

Cabillaud – Cod. Also *Morue*.

Caen (*à la Mode de Caen*) – Tripe cooked in cider and calvados and seasoned with garlic and various spices.

Caille – Quail.

Calmar – Calamary – squid.

Camerani – Poultry or calf's sweetbreads garnished with macaroni, tartlets filled with *foie gras*, shredded truffles and slices of pickled tongue.

Canapés – Small rectangular pieces of toasted bread on which are spread various delicacies, either for garnishing winged game or as appetizers.

Canard – Duck.

Cancalaise (*à la Cancalaise*) – A fish garnish of oysters and shrimps in Normande sauce.

Caneton – Duckling.

Cantaloupe – Melon. The name originates from Cantaloupo, near Rome.

Câpres – Capers.

Cardinal (*à la Cardinal*) – Fish served with mushrooms and slices of truffle. Also fruit topped with raspberry syrup and sprinkled with shredded almonds.

Cardon – Cardoon. A plant similar to the artichoke. Only the stems are eaten.

Cari – Curry.

Carmin – Carmine. Non-toxic, vivid scarlet colouring matter made from cochineal, used in decorating various preparations.

Carpe – Carp.

Carré – *Carré d'agneau* – loin of lamb.

Carrelet – Plaice.

Cassata – A light Neapolitan ice cream served in slices.

Cassis – Blackcurrant.

Casserole – A large type of saucepan made in fireproof porcelain, terracotta, or in a variety of metals which is usually decorative enough to use as a serving dish. *Also* a dish served in rice shaped like a casserole, or potatoes shaped in a casserole.

Cassoulet – A bean stew cooked with duck, goose, mutton or pork.

Castiglione (*à la Castiglione*) – A garnish of aubergines sautéed in butter, mushrooms stuffed with rice and slices of poached beef marrow.

Catalane (*à la Catalane*) – Aubergines sautéed in oil and pilaf of rice served with large pieces of meat.

Cavour (*à la Cavour*) – Sweetbreads, veal escalopes or small pieces of meat dressed on small circles of polenta, garnished with slices of truffle, and mushrooms stuffed with chicken liver purée.

Cèpes – Boletus – large edible mushrooms.

Cerfeuil – Chervil.

Cerise – Cherry.

Cervelas – Short sausage made with pork meat, pork fat and garlic.

Cervelle – Brains.

Chalonnaise (*à la Chalonnaise*) – Poultry or calves' sweet-breads garnished with tartlets of cocks' kidneys, cocks' combs, truffles and mushrooms.

Chambord – Braised fish garnished with fish *quenelles*, fillets of sole, sautéed soft roes, fresh-water crayfish, truffles, mushrooms and fried croûtons with a red wine sauce.

Champignons – Mushrooms.

Chanoinesse – Chicken, sweetbreads or poached eggs garnished with small carrots in cream and truffles, served with a sherry sauce.

Chanterelle – A species of edible mushroom.

Chantilly – (1) *Crème chantilly*: Fresh cream beaten to a light frothy mousse, sweetened and sometimes flavoured with vanilla or other essences.

(2) *À la Chantilly*: A sweet served with Chantilly cream *or* roast chicken stuffed with rice and *foie gras* and truffles and served with *foie gras* and truffles over which is poured Chantilly cream.

Chasseur (*à la Chasseur*) – A garnish of sliced mushrooms sautéed and flavoured with shallots and moistened with white wine served with fowl, small pieces of meat or eggs.

Châteaubriand – A thick slice of grilled fillet steak.

Châtelaine (*à la Châtelaine*) – Large cuts of meat garnished with artichoke hearts stuffed with chestnut purée and rice, potato balls and braised lettuce.

Chatouillard – A kind of chipped potato.

Chaud-froid – Fowl or game cooked as a hot dish but served cold.

Chausson – A turnover.

Cheveux d'ange – A very fine type of vermicelli.

Chicorée. Endive. In America this is known as Chicory, but chicory in English is equivalent to the French endive, a great confusion of words. To simplify: The French *Chicorée* is the English *endive*, which is a curly-leaved salad plant, usually eaten as a salad, with oil and vinegar, French dressing, etc.

Chiffonade – Vegetables, cut into strips before cooking, used as a garnish for thick and clear soups.

Chinonaise (à la Chinonaise) – Large cuts of meat garnished with green cabbage, stuffed with braised sausage meat, and potatoes sprinkled with parsley.

Choesels – A Belgian tripe stew.

Choron – A Béarnaise sauce with concentrated tomato purée added.

Chou – Cabbage. Also a cream puff.

Chou-fleur – Cauliflower.

Choucroute – Sauerkraut.

Ciboulet – Chives.

Cingalaise – A cold sauce composed of a *salpicon* of hard-boiled eggs, tomatoes, cooked cucumber, curry, oil, lemon juice, chives and parsley.

Citron – Lemon.

Civet – Game stew.

Clamart (à la Clamart) – Large or small cuts of meat garnished with artichoke hearts filled with peas, served with potato balls.

Clermont (à la Clermont) – Large cuts of meat garnished with braised cabbage, pickled pork and potatoes.

Collioure – A cold sauce composed of mayonnaise laced with garlic, purée of anchovies and parsley.

Comfits – Vegetables or fruit preserved in sugar, brandy or vinegar. Not to be confused with CoNfit.

Compôte – Fresh or dried fruit cooked in syrup and served cold.

Comtesse Riguidi – See *Riguidi*.

Concombre – Cucumber.

Confit – Pork, duck or goose cooked in its own fat then placed in a terrine covered by the same fat for preservation.

Confiture – Jam.

Consommé – A concentrated and clarified meat stock often served as a hot clear soup or a cold jelly soup.

Conti (à la Conti) – Small cuts of meat garnished with croquettes of lentil purée and fried potato balls, served with a Madeira sauce.

Coq – Cock, but implying chicken in most dishes.

Coquille St Jacques – Scallops.

Cornichon – Gherkin.

Côtelettes – Chops.

Court-Bouillon – An aromatic liquid in which fish, meat or vegetables are cooked.

Courge – Vegetable marrow.

Courgette – Italian marrow.

Cous-cous – A North African dish made of crushed rice or millet flour, mutton, chicken and vegetables.

Crapaudine (à la Crapaudine) – Grilled pigeon, or other fowl, served with gherkins.

Crécy (à la Crécy) – Soups and broths prepared with carrots.

Crème (à la Crème) – Meat and vegetables served with the juices mixed with cream.

Créole (à la Créole) – Dishes served with rice pilaf and garnished with pimentos and tomatoes. When referring to a sweet – also served with rice, and orange.

Crêpe – Pancake.

Crépinettes – Round, flat sausages enveloped in caul – paunch membrane.

Cresson – Watercress.

Cressonnière – A cold sauce composed of crushed hard-boiled eggs mixed with watercress and oil.

Crevettes – Shrimps.

Croissant – A crescent-shaped roll made of leavened dough or light pastry.

Croque au Sel (à la Croque au Sel) – Vegetables eaten raw with salt.

Crustaces – Crustaceans. Crabs, lobsters, shrimps, etc.

Croustade – Pastry.

Croûtons – Small cubes of bread fried in butter, generally served with thick soups.

Cussy (à la Cussy) – Poultry or small cuts of meat garnished with artichokes stuffed with mushroom purée, cocks' kidneys, and shredded truffles. Served with Madeira or Port sauce.

*

Daumont (à la Daumont) – Large fish garnished with Nantua sauce, soft roes, fresh water crayfish tails, mushrooms and *quenelles*.

Dauphine (à la Dauphine) – Potatoes, mashed, rolled into balls and deep fried.

Demi-Deuil – Poached poultry or sweetbreads, braised in a white sauce, served with truffles. The dish is black and white, hence the name, which means 'half mourning'.

Demi-Glace – A Madeira- or Sherry-flavoured brown sauce.

Demoiselles d'Honneur – Maids of honour – little cakes.

Diable (à la Diable) – Grilled poultry sprinkled with breadcrumbs, served with Diable sauce – a white wine sauce mixed with cayenne pepper, vinegar, shallots, thyme, bay leaf, and parsley.

Dieppoise (à la Dieppoise) – Fish cooked in white wine served with crayfish tails and mussels in a white wine sauce.

Dijonnaise – A cold sauce composed of crushed hard-boiled eggs, Dijon mustard beaten with oil and lemon juice.

Dinde – Turkey.

Diplomat – A *velouté* sauce of lobster stock, mushrooms and brandy, sometimes mixed with diced truffles.

Dorade – Sea bream.

Dubarry (à la Dubarry) – Large or small cuts of meat garnished with cauliflower cheese and Mornay sauce.

Duchesse (à la Duchesse) – Dishes served with *Pomme duchesse* – mashed potatoes.

Duroc – Sautéed poultry and small cuts of meat garnished with new potatoes.

Duxelles – Small cuts of meat garnished with mushrooms pounded into a hash with onions and shallots cooked in a white wine.

*

Écarlate (à l'Écarlate) – Cooked ox tongue wrapped in lard, threaded into an ox bladder which is painted with carmine. Served cold as a buffet dish.

Échalotes – Shallots.

Écrevisse – Freshwater crayfish.

Émincé – Thinly sliced braised or roast meat left-overs, served with a substantial sauce.

Endive – Chicory. A firm white-leaved plant served cooked or finely chopped and eaten cold as a salad. See *Chicorée*.

Entrecôte – A steak cut from between two ribs of beef.

Épaule – Shoulder.

Épices – Spices.

Épinard – Spinach.

Escargots – Snails.

Estragon – Tarragon.

Esturgeon – Sturgeon.

Étuvée – Food cooked in a tightly closed container with the minimum of liquid.

*

Faisan – Pheasant.

Farce – Stuffing.

Favart – Poultry garnished with chicken *quenelles*, and *salpicon* of mushroom tartlets.

Favorite (*à la Favorite*) – Large and small cuts of meat garnished with braised artichokes, braised lettuce, mushrooms, mixed diced vegetables and Anna potatoes.

Fenouil – Fennel.

Fermière (*à la Fermière*) – Braised meats garnished with carrots, celery, onions and turnips cooked in butter.

Fève – Broad bean.

Figue – Fig.

Filet Mignon – A small cut taken from the end of a beef fillet, grilled or sautéed.

Financière (*à la Financière*) – Poultry and meat dishes garnished with *quenelles*, sweetbreads, cocks' combs, cocks' kidneys, olives, truffles and mushrooms.

Fines Herbes (*aux Fines Herbes*) – A preparation containing chopped parsley.

Flageolet – Small, white, kidney bean.

Flamande (*à la Flamande*) – A hot-pot of large cuts of meat,

diced belly of pork, carrots, braised cabbage and potatoes.
Asparagus à la Flamande are served hot with butter and
halves of hot hard-boiled eggs, which should be mashed
with butter before eating.

Florentine (à la Florentine) – Fish or eggs served on buttered
stewed spinach, covered with Mornay sauce and sprinkled
with grated Gruyère.

Foie – Liver.

Fondue – Cheese melted in white wine, seasoned with pepper and kirsch, heated in a casserole which is placed in the
centre of the table over a spirit lamp. Guests dip cubes of
bread into the mixture, eating the fondue direct from the
casserole. *Also* – Vegetable Fondue, various vegetables
cooked in butter till they are reduced to a purée.

Forestière (à la Forestière) – Meat and poultry dishes garnished with morels, bacon and fried potatoes.

Fraise – Strawberry.

Framboise – Raspberry.

Française (à la Française) – Large cuts of meat garnished
with *duchesse* potatoes filled with diced mixed vegetables,
asparagus tips, braised lettuce and cauliflower coated with
Hollandaise sauce.

Frangipane – A cream puff pastry made with flour, yolks of
egg, butter and milk, used in fish and poultry stuffings.

Frascati (à la Frascati) – Meat dishes garnished with slices of
foie gras, asparagus tips, mushrooms and truffles.

Friandises – Sweets.

Fricassée – A method of preparing poultry in a white sauce.

Fumets – Liquids used for flavouring which are prepared by
boiling down certain foods in stock or wine.

*

Galette – Large round cake of flaky pastry.

Gâteau – Cake.

Gaude – A maize-flour porridge, similar to the polenta.

Gauloise (*à la Gauloise*) – *Vol-au-vents* garnished with cocks' kidneys, pickled tongues, truffles and a Madeira-flavoured sauce. *Also* a clear soup served with cocks' combs and kidneys.

Gelées – Jellies.

Genevoise – A sauce served with fish cooked in a *court-bouillon*.

Genoese – A type of cake.

Gibier – Game. All edible wild birds and animals.

Gigot – Leg. *Gigot d'agneau* – leg of lamb.

Girofle – Clove.

Glaces – Ice cream.

Gnocchi – Small, walnut-shaped balls of cooked flour or semolina served with grated Parmesan.

Godard – Poultry and large cuts of meat garnished with veal or poultry *quenelles* with truffles, braised sweetbreads, cocks' combs and kidneys, truffles and mushrooms.

Gorenflot – Large braised cuts of meat garnished with saveloy sausages, potatoes *à la ménagère* and braised red cabbage. Served with a Madeira sauce.

Goujon – Gudgeon.

Gratin (*au Gratin*) – Fish browned under the grill or in the oven.

Grecque (*à la Grecque*) – Vegetables (usually artichokes or aubergines) boiled in a special mixture of water, olive oil, lemon juice with thyme, bay leaf, fennel, celery, and coriander as a seasoning.

Grenouille – Frog.

Gribiche – A cold sauce for fish composed of hard-boiled egg yolks beaten to a mayonnaise with oil and vinegar, then seasoned with capers, chopped gherkins, chervil, tarragon and parsley.

Grillade – Grill.

Grive – Thrush.

Groseille – Currant.

*

Hareng – Herring.

Helder – Small sautéed cuts of meat garnished with a thick tomato fondue, Béarnaise sauce and potato balls.

Henri IV – Small cuts of meat garnished with artichoke hearts filled with Béarnaise sauce, shredded truffles and potato balls. Served with Madeira sauce.

Hollandaise – A hot sauce served with fish, vegetables and eggs, composed of yolks of egg and butter.

Holstein – Escalope of veal, breadcrumbed, sautéed in butter and topped with a fried egg.

Hongroise (à la Hongroise) – Meat, fish and eggs, cooked in a cream sauce seasoned with paprika.

Hôtelière (à l'Hôtelière) – Fish sautéed in butter, garnished with chopped mushrooms mixed with *demi-glace*, butter and *fines herbes*. *Also* a thick soup made with purée of potato, lentils and beans bound with cream. Served with croûtons.

Huile – Oil.

Huîtres – Oysters.

*

Impératrice (à l'Impératrice) – Desserts served with vanilla-flavoured rice, crystallized fruit soaked in kirsch and whipped cream.

Impériale (à l'Impériale) – Dishes garnished with *foie gras*, truffles, cocks' combs and kidneys.

Indienne (à l'Indienne) – Dishes garnished with curried rice or rice and curry sauce.

Italienne (à l'Italienne) – Meat, poultry, fish or vegetable dishes served with finely chopped mushrooms.

Ivoire (à l'Ivoire) – Chicken served with a *suprême* sauce, mushrooms and *quenelles*.

*

Jalousies – Little cakes of flaky pastry.

Jambon – Ham.

Japonaise – Dishes which include Chinese artichokes. *Salade Japonaise*, however, is made with mussels, truffles and potatoes.

Jardinière (à la Jardinière) – Braised, roasted or stewed meats and poultry served with fresh vegetables.

Jessica – Veal escalopes, chicken or poached eggs, garnished with artichokes stuffed with a *salpicon* of bone marrow, shallots and morels. Served with Anna potatoes.

Joinville (à la Joinville) – Poached fillet of sole garnished with shrimps, truffles and mushrooms. This dish is usually carefully presented so that the sole fillets are arranged in a circle with the ends pointing upwards on the tips of which peeled pink shrimps are balanced.

Julienne – A clear vegetable soup to which a mixture of finely shredded vegetables cooked in butter is added.

Jus – Juice, meat-juice.

*

Kebab – Turkish name for dishes which include skewered meats.

*

Lait – Milk.

Laitance – Soft roe.

Laitue – Lettuce.

Langouste – Crawfish.

Langoustines – Dublin Bay prawns. Now, for some reason, found more acceptable under their Italian name of *scampi*.

Langues de Chat – Thin, flat, narrow, crisp, dry biscuits.

Languedocienne (*à la Languedocienne*) – Dishes garnished with aubergines, *cèpes*, tomatoes, and garlic-flavoured sauce.

Lapereau – Young wild rabbit.

Lapin – Rabbit.

Légumes – Vegetables.

Liégeoise (*à la Liégeoise*) – Meat dishes cooked with crushed juniper berries.

Lièvre – Hare.

Limousine (*à la Limousine*) – Meat or poultry served with red cabbage.

Lorraine (*à la Lorraine*) – Large braised cuts of meat garnished with red cabbage braised in red wine and *fondantes* potatoes.

Lucullus – Dishes cooked with *foie gras* and truffles.

Lyonnaise (*à la Lyonnaise*) – Large cuts of meat garnished with onions and braised *fondantes* potatoes.

*

Macédoine – A mixture of vegetables or fruit, served hot or cold, cooked or fresh.

Mâconnaise (*à la Mâconnaise*) – Various meat dishes flavoured with red wine.

Madeleine – A small plain cake made with flour, eggs, butter and sugar.

Madrilène (*à la Madrilène*) – Dishes flavoured with tomato juice or clear soups flavoured with tomato juice and usually served chilled.

Maillot – Ham or large cuts of meat garnished with French beans, braised lettuce, onions, cauliflower, carrots and turnips, served with a Madeira-flavoured sauce.

Maintenon (*à la Maintenon*) – Dishes served with a mixture of onions and rice purée, bechamel sauce, shredded mushrooms and truffles.

Maison – A term indicating that the dish is prepared by the owner of the restaurant, or his chef, and based on a recipe which he can claim to have invented.

Maître d'Hôtel (*Beurre Maître d'Hôtel*) – Creamed butter with chopped parsley, lemon juice, salt and pepper, served with grilled meat and fish.

Malossol – A quality of grading in caviare denoting the salt content.

Maquereau – Mackerel.

Maraichère (*à la Maraichère*) – Roast or braised meats served with small onions, carrots, braised stuffed cucumbers, artichokes, château potatoes, carrots, small onions, and salsify.

Maréchale (*à la Maréchale*) – Small cuts of meat and poultry dipped in egg, breadcrumbed and fried in butter, garnished with asparagus tips and truffles.

Marengo – Chicken or veal served with crayfish, tomatoes, garlic, brandy and sauce.

Marigny (*à la Marigny*) – Small cuts of meat garnished with artichoke hearts, stuffed with corn kernels in cream, browned potato balls and white wine sauce.

Marinière (à la Marinière) – Fish dishes cooked in white-wine sauce with mussels and a *velouté* sauce.

Marivaux – Large cuts of meat garnished with *duchesse* potatoes filled with finely chopped celery, artichoke hearts, carrots, mushrooms sprinkled with Parmesan cheese and served with French beans.

Marocaine (à la Marocaine) – Lamb garnished with saffron-seasoned rice pilaf, braised pimentos filled with chicken stuffing and diced marrow, served with a light tomato juice sauce.

Marrons – Chestnuts.

Mascotte (à la Mascotte) – Small cuts of meat and poultry garnished with sautéed artichoke hearts and small potatoes cooked in butter.

Massena (à la Massena) – Steak fillet garnished with artichoke hearts filled with thick Béarnaise sauce and strips of poached beef marrow.

Massenet – Large or small cuts of meat garnished with Anna potatoes, small artichoke hearts filled with a *salpicon* of bone marrow, served with French beans and a Madeira sauce.

Massepain – Marzipan.

Matelote – A fresh-water fish stew made with red or white wine.

Matignon – Large or small cuts of meat garnished with artichoke hearts, filled with a vegetable fondue, served with braised lettuce and a Madeira or Port-wine sauce.

Médaillons – Meats, sometimes fish, cut in the shape of medallions, round, small, flat, for presentation.

Melba – Large or small cuts of meat garnished with truffles, mushrooms, braised lettuce, small tomatoes stuffed with a *salpicon* of chicken stuffing and served with a Port-flavoured sauce. *Also* fruit served with vanilla ice-cream and thick raspberry syrup.

Mentonnaise (*à la Mentonnaise*) – Rock-pool fish cooked and seasoned with black olives, tomatoes and garlic.

Merlan – Whiting.

Meunière (*à la Meunière*) – Fish lightly flavoured, fried in butter sprinkled with parsley and lemon juice.

Mexicaine (*à la Mexicaine*) – Fried lamb chops garnished with banana fritters.

Mikado – Escalopes of veal or chicken garnished with small tartlets of soya-bean shoots and curried rice.

Milanaise (*à la Milanaise*) – Meat, fish and vegetables, dipped in egg, breadcrumbed, mixed with Parmesan cheese and fried in butter, served with macaroni, garnished with tomato sauce, Gruyère and Parmesan cheese, shredded ham, pickled tongue and truffles.

Mille Feuilles – A pastry. Many layers of cream and jam separated by as many layers of thin, flaky pastry.

Mimosa – A salad on which is sprinkled shredded hard yolks of egg – resembling mimosa.

Minute – Small cuts of meat sautéed in sizzling butter for one minute – or as briskly as possible.

Mirabeau (*à la Mirabeau*) – Grilled meat garnished with anchovy fillets, olives and tarragon leaves.

Miroir (*au Miroir*) – Eggs baked in the oven so that the white forms a polished film over the yolk.

Mode (*à la Mode*) – Large cuts of braised beef, cooked with white wine and brandy.

Moelle – Bone marrow.

Moka – A strong coffee made with beans from Mocha in Arabia.

Monselet (*à la Monselet*) – Dishes garnished with truffles, artichoke hearts and fried potatoes.

Mont Bry – Small cuts of meat, garnished with *cèpes* in cream and *canapés* of spinach coated in Parmesan.

Montmorency (*à la Montmorency*) – Dishes, entrées or entremets, served with cherries.

Montpensier – Chicken or small cuts of meat garnished with sliced truffles and asparagus tips.

Morel – A black-pointed edible fungus which grows in the spring on the fringe of woods.

Mornay (*à la Mornay*) – Dishes covered with Mornay sauce composed of cream, butter, Gruyère and Parmesan cheese.

Mortadella – A large, melon-shaped Italian cooked pork sausage, mainly served as hors d'œuvre.

Morue – Salt cod.

Moules – Mussels.

Mousquetaire – A cold sauce composed of a mayonnaise laced with white wine, chopped shallots seasoned with cayenne pepper.

Mousseline – Various preparations with whipped cream added.

Mouton – Mutton.

Musette (*en Musette*) – A braised joint of beef rolled in the form of a bladder.

*

Nage (*à la Nage*) – Shellfish cooked in a *court-bouillon* and flavoured with herbs. Served hot or cold.

Nanette – Lamb cutlets, veal escalopes or calf's sweetbreads garnished with small artichoke hearts with creamed lettuce and mushrooms stuffed with a *salpicon* of truffles.

Nantua (*à la Nantua*) – Dishes garnished with freshwater crayfish and covered with crayfish purée.

Navet – Turnip.

Newburg – Hot lobster cooked in a sherry sauce, served with a thick, rich, cream sauce.

Nichette – Small cuts of meat garnished with grilled mushrooms filled with grated horseradish, cocks' combs and cocks' kidneys in a bone-marrow sauce.

Niçoise – Various dishes prepared and served with olive oil, tomatoes and anchovies.

Nivernaise (*à la Nivernaise*) – Meat dishes served with small carrots and glazed onions.

Noisettes d'Agneau – Pieces of meat taken from the loin of lamb and trimmed into round, thick fillets.

Noix – Nut.

Normande (*à la Normande*) – Fish braised in white wine, garnished with poached oysters, shrimps, mushrooms, truffles, fried gudgeon, freshwater crayfish, and lozenge-shaped pieces of bread fried in butter. Mussels are also sometimes added. *Also* small cuts of meat and winged game bathed in cider and served with calvados-enriched sauce.

Norvégienne (*à la Norvégienne*) – Ice-cream. A surprise dessert of ice-cream inside a hot soufflé or pastry casing.

Nouilles – Noodles.

Noyau – The soft, edible part within the hard shell of a nut or fruit stone. The fruit kernel.

*

Ocietrova – Caviare. From the medium-sized species of the sturgeon, *Ocietrova*. Medium grain.

Œuf – Egg.

Oie – Goose.

Oignon – Onion.

Oreiller de la Belle Aurore – An elaborate square game pie, served cold.

Orge – Barley.

Orientale (à l'Orientale) – Fish, vegetable and egg dishes cooked with tomatoes and flavoured with saffron and garlic.

Orly (à la Orly) – Deep fried filleted fish served with a tomato sauce.

Oseille – Sorrel.

*

Paella – A Spanish rice dish cooked in oil with vegetables and/or chicken, meat, other vegetables.

Pain – Bread.

Paloise (à la Paloise) – Grilled meat garnished simply with buttered French beans and potato balls.

Pamplemousse – Grapefruit.

Panais – Parsnip.

Paner – To 'breadcrumb' meat, fish or vegetables, before frying in butter.

Parfaits – Light ices of varying flavours.

Parisienne (à la Parisienne) – Meat and poultry garnished with Parisienne potatoes.

Parmentier – Dishes which include potatoes which have been cooked with the dish itself.

Parmesane (à la Parmesane) – A variety of dishes which include grated Parmesan cheese.

Paupiettes – Thin slices of meat or fillets of fish, stuffed with a stuffing, rolled into the shape of a sausage, wrapped in rashers of bacon and braised.

Pavé – A square mould of meat or fish mousse in aspic, topped with truffle decorations, or a square-shaped sponge cake topped with varying creams.

Paysanne (*à la Paysanne*) – Braised meat and poultry garnished with fried bacon, turnips, celery, onions, carrots and potatoes.

Pêche – Peach.

Perdreau – Partridge.

Périgourdine (*à la Périgourdine*) – Dishes served with *Périgueux* sauce and *foie gras*.

Périgueux – A truffle sauce served with small cuts of meat, game, fowl and *vol-au-vent*.

Persane (*à la Persane*) – Lamb cutlets garnished with sautéed aubergines, fried onions and fondue of tomato and pimentos.

Persil – Parsley.

Petits Fours – Small fancy cakes and biscuits.

Piémontaise (*à la Piémontaise*) – Meat and poultry garnished with risotto, mixed with truffles.

Pilaf – Lightly cooked rice to which various ingredients are added – chicken, shellfish, lobster, shrimps, sweetbreads, kidneys, etc.

Piment – Pimento.

Pipérade – A purée of tomatoes and pimentos cooked with eggs.

Pissaladière – A savoury tart with cooked onions, anchovies and black olive fillings.

Pistache – Pistachio. *En Pistache* – Meat garnished only with cloves of garlic *not* pistachios.

Pistou – A vegetable broth with a basis of powdered garlic, grilled tomatoes, oil, basil, and vermicelli.

Poireau – Leek.

Poire – Pear.

Pois – Pea.

Poitrine – Belly.

Poivre – Pepper.

Polenta – Cold maize meal porridge cooked in the oven and cut into flat squares or lozenge-shaped slices. Used to garnish various meat and fish dishes.

Polonaise (*à la Polonaise*) – Vegetables garnished with hard yolks of egg, parsley and melted butter.

Pomme – Apple.

Pomme de Terre – Potato. Sometimes referred to as simply 'Pomme', however, e.g. *Pomme duchesse*.

Portugaise – A tomato paste made with oil and flavoured with garlic, onion and parsley.

Potage – Soup, broth.

Poularde – A fat hen or roasting chicken, weighing from 3½ lb.

Poulet – Chicken, weighing from 1½ to 3½ lb.

Poulette (*à la Poulette*) – A fricassée of previously cooked offal mixed with cream, egg, yolk, *velouté* sauce and garnished with mushrooms and onions.

Poussin – A very young chicken.

Praline – An almond coated with very sweet coloured sugar.

Pré Salé – The meat of young sheep which have been fed in aromatic pastures.

Prince Albert – Fillet of beef stuffed with *foie gras*, garnished with truffles and served with a Madeira or Port flavoured sauce.

Princesse (*à la Princesse*) – Dishes garnished with asparagus tips and truffles.

Printanière (*à la Printanière*) – Meat dishes garnished with spring vegetables.

Profiterole – A small, round éclair pastry filled with game purées, cheese mixtures or sweet cream, jams or custard.

Provençale – Various dishes from Provence, most of which have a garlic base.

Prune – Plum.

Pruneau – Prune.

*

Quenelles – Types of dumpling made with stuffings of varying meats, poultry, game, fish and crustaceans, bound with egg.

Quiche – A savoury custard tart.

*

Radis – Radish.

Ragoût – A stew.

Raifort – Horseradish.

Raisin – Grape.

Ravigotte – A highly seasoned white sauce which is served either hot or cold.

Régence – Poultry, veal, sweetbreads, garnished with chicken *quenelles*, sautéed *foie gras*, mushrooms, cocks' combs, and truffles.

Réjane – Braised veal, sweetbreads, garnished with *duchesse* potatoes, filled with leaf spinach, artichokes, and poached bone marrow.

Rémoulade – An elaborate mayonnaise to which is added capers, gherkins, spring onions, chervil, tarragon, parsley, and anchovy essence.

Renaissance (à la Renaissance) – Roast meats presented on the plate surrounded by neat little heaps of mixed vegetables.

Riche (à la Riche) – Fish garnished with diplomat sauce.

Richelieu (à la Richelieu) – Dishes garnished with braised lettuce, mushrooms, tomatoes, and lightly roasted potatoes.

Riguidi (Escargots Comtesse Riguidi) – Snail shells filled with fillets of anchovy, or lambs' sweetbreads, or finely chopped veal, chicken, fish, mixed with truffles, cream, etc. An imitation snail, in fact.

Ris – Sweetbreads.

Riz – Rice.

Rognon – Kidney.

Romaine (à la Romaine) – Large cuts of meat garnished with spinach and Anna potatoes served with tomato sauce.

Romanov – Meat garnished with sliced cucumbers stuffed with chopped mushrooms, served with *duchesse* potatoes sprinkled with horseradish sauce.

Romarin – Rosemary.

Rossini – Small cuts of meat garnished with a slice of sautéed *foie gras* and thick slices of truffles served with a Madeira sauce.

Rôti – Roast.

Rouget – Red mullet.

Roux – A mixture of butter and flour cooked together to serve as a thickening element in sauces.

Royale (*à la Royale*) – Poached poultry coated with a *velouté* sauce garnished with truffle purée.

*

Sagan – Chicken, veal escalopes or sweetbreads garnished with risotto, mushrooms stuffed with a *salpicon* of brain and truffles, served with a Madeira sauce.

Saint Germain – A thick pea soup or a garnish of fresh peas. *Filets de Sole Saint Germain*, however, are sole fillets coated with breadcrumbs, buttered and lightly grilled, with a Béarnaise sauce, and *noisette* potatoes, not necessarily served with peas.

Saint Honoré – A rich, round pastry filled with cream and topped with crystallized fruits.

Saint Saens – Poultry garnished with asparagus tips, fritters of *foie gras* and truffles and cocks' kidneys.

Salami – Specially prepared, dried and salted pork or beef sausage, eaten raw and cold as hors d'œuvres.

Salpicon – A number of edible ingredients cut into small dice and bound with a sauce, served as a garnish, hot or cold.

Salsify – Oyster plant.

Saltimbocca alla Romana – An Italian dish which is becoming popular. Small pieces of veal, covered with thin, smoked ham, a leaf of sage, cooked in butter and marsala wine.

Sardalaise – A cold sauce composed of hard-boiled egg yolks, fresh cream, truffles, oil, lemon and Armagnac.

Sarde (*à la Sarde*) – Large cuts of meat garnished with croquettes of rice and cheese, mushrooms and French beans served with a thin tomato sauce.

Sarrasine (*à la Sarrasine*) – Large cuts of meat garnished with rice tartlets filled with tomato fondue, onion and buck-wheat cakes.

Saucisse – Sausage.

Saucisson – A variety of sausages served cold.

Sauté – Ingredients cooked in a wide, shallow frying pan, in butter or oil.

Savarin – A cake soaked in a syrup, rum or kirsch.

Scampi – Dublin Bay prawns.

Serge – Escalopes of veal dipped in chopped truffles and mushrooms, garnished with artichokes and shredded ham simmered in Madeira.

Serviette (*à la Serviette*) – Various cooked foods served in a folded napkin, e.g. truffles cooked in hot ashes, baked potatoes, etc.

Sevruga – Caviare. The smallest of the sturgeon species, the *Sevruga*, from which the smallest grain is obtained.

Sicilienne (*à la Sicilienne*) – Fish soup mixed with cream and yolks of egg.

Sorbet – Sherbet – or water ice.

Soubise – A purée of onions and rice served with large or small cuts of meat.

Soufflé – A delicate savoury or sweet dish of varying flavours made of stiffly beaten whites of egg mixed to other ingredients, puffed up when cooked in the oven.

Sous Cloche – Ingredients cooked under a cover. Literal translation – under a bell.

Strasbourgeoise (*à la Strasbourgeoise*) – Pot-roasted or braised poultry garnished with braised sauerkraut, slices of *foie gras* and salt pork.

Sultane (*à la Sultane*) – Chicken garnished with canapés of chicken stuffing, cocks' combs, truffle tartlets and bleached pistachio nuts served with a slightly curried sauce.

Suprême – The breast and wings of chicken or game birds, removed when raw and cooked in various preparations.

Suzette (*Crêpe Suzette*) – Pancake coated with vanilla-flavoured sugar, lemon juice and Grand Marnier, folded in two and rolled. Usually set alight before the customer by the waiter to add a little drama to the meal and also to brown the pancake slightly.

*

Talleyrand – A chicken *velouté* sauce to which is added fresh cream, truffles, diced tongue and madeira.

Tartare – (1) *À la Tartare* – Raw minced beef steak seasoned with capers, chopped onions, parsley, salt and pepper, and topped with a raw egg yolk; (2) A mayonnaise made with crushed hard egg yolks, oil and chives.

Thermidor – Roasted lobster meat covered with a rich béchamel sauce laced with white wine, seasoned with chervil, tarragon and shallots, served in the split halves of the shell, sprinkled with Parmesan cheese and lightly browned in the oven.

Thon – Tunny.

Topinambour – Jerusalem artichoke.

Tortue – (1) Turtle; (2) *En Tortue* – Calves' heads garnished with olives, mushrooms, truffles, gherkins, veal *quenelles*, freshwater crayfish, calves' brain, calves' tongue, and fried bread.

Toscane (*à la Toscane*) – Breast of chicken or veal escalopes dipped in grated Parmesan, garnished with a mixture of diced mushrooms, *foie gras*, and truffles sautéed in butter.

Toulousaine (*à la Toulousaine*) – Poached or roast poultry served with a ragoût bound with white sauce.

Tournedos – Slices from the heart of a beef fillet.

Trouvillaise (*à la Trouvillaise*) – Fish garnished with mussels, shelled shrimps, and mushrooms, served with a shrimp sauce.

Tyrolienne (*à la Tyrolienne*) – Grilled meats with tomatoes cooked in butter, fried onions, served with thick veal gravy.

*

Valenciennes (*à la Valenciennes*) – Poultry or small cuts of meat garnished with rice mixed with a *salpicon* of pimentos.

Valois (*à la Valois*) – Dishes served with a Valois sauce – a Béarnaise finished off with meat glaze and artichoke hearts.

Veau – Veal.

Velouté – A thick white sauce made with veal or chicken stock.

Venetienne – A green soup made with fish *velouté*, herbs, pounded spinach and white wine.

Vert Pré – Grilled meats garnished with straw potatoes, watercress, and topped with *Maître d'Hôtel* butter.

Vichy (*à la Vichy*) – Carrots cooked in Vichy water.

Victoria – Small cuts of meat garnished with artichokes, tomatoes, stuffed with mushroom purée, and served with a Madeira or Port sauce.

Viennoise (*à la Viennoise*) – Poultry or small cuts of meat garnished with anchovy fillets, olives, capers, chopped hard-boiled eggs, served with a hot butter sauce.

Vierge – Boiled vegetables served with frothy butter whipped up with salt, pepper and lemon juice.

Villeroi (à la Villeroi) – Meat, fish, eggs or vegetables coated with a mushroom, tomato or truffle sauce, then breadcrumbed and fried in deep fat.

Vinaigre – Vinegar.

Vinaigrette – Cold oil and vinegar sauce seasoned with salt and pepper and chopped herbs.

Vincent – Cold sauce of mayonnaise, chopped hard-boiled eggs and herbs.

Vladimir – Small cuts of meat garnished with lengths of cucumber simmered in butter and diced vegetable marrow, and served with sour cream sauce blended with paprika and grated horseradish.

Volaille – Poultry.

Volière (en Volière) – An elaborate way of presenting cooked birds, with the head, outspread wings and tail re-fixed with little wooden pegs to the cooked bird.

*

Walewska (à la Walewska) – Poached fish garnished with truffles and coated with Mornay sauce.

Winterthur (à la Winterthur) – Crayfish stuffed with peeled shrimps and *salpicon* of crayfish.

*

Zabaglione – A sweet cream mousse composed of whipped yolks of egg, sugar, wine, and flavoured with vanilla, orange, lemon or tangerine.

Potatoes – *Pommes de Terre*

Allumettes – Cut like matchsticks and fried.

à l' Alsacienne – New potatoes cooked in a broth with lean bacon and button onions.

à l' Anglaise – Peeled and boiled in salted water.

Anna – Raw, peeled, cut in round slices, ranged in layers, covered in butter, and cooked in the oven.

Berni – Mashed, mixed with chopped truffles, grilled almonds, raw egg yolks, butter, shaped into croquettes, breadcrumbed, and fried.

Berrichonne – Egg-shaped, cooked in consommé, with sliced onions, and bacon.

au Beurre – Egg-shaped, cooked in the oven with butter.

Bonne Femme – Egg-shaped, cooked in butter with onions, in the oven.

à la Bordelaise – Sliced, tossed in butter with onions, beef marrow, and a little garlic.

à la Boulangère – Baked in the oven with sliced onions, butter, and bathed in consommé.

à la Bretonne – Cut into cubes, stewed in consommé with chopped tomatoes, onions, garlic, and parsley.

Brioches – Mashed, shaped into brioches and browned in the oven.

Brunes-Hachées – Boiled, chopped when cold and tossed in butter till brown.

Cendrillon – Baked, scooped out of their skins, mixed with cream and butter, replaced in their half-jackets, sprinkled with cheese, and browned in the oven.

Chambéry – Sliced, boiled, browned in the oven between layers of grated cheese.

Chateau – Egg-shaped, cooked in butter, and browned in the oven.

Châtouillard – Large and long, specially cut into a spiral shape, forming a circle, fried as 'soufflé' potatoes.

Chester – Mashed with salt, pepper, nutmeg, and yolks of eggs, mixed with grated Cheshire cheese.

Chips – Cut into round thin slices and fried in deep fat.

Copeaux – Cut as shavings and fried crisp.

à la Crème – Boiled, peeled, sliced, cooked in butter, and served with cream.

Croquettes – Mashed, mixed with butter, egg yolks, shaped into flat balls, breadcrumbed, and fried.

Dauphine – Mashed, mixed with puff pastry, butter, egg yolks, shaped into flat balls, breadcrumbed, and fried.

Dauphinoise (*à la Dauphinoise*) – Sliced buttered potatoes cooked in the oven with melted Gruyère cheese, grated nutmeg, and garlic.

Delmonico – Boiled, peeled, cut into cubes and stewed with milk, butter, cream, sprinkled with grated cheese, and browned in the oven.

Denier (*en Denier*) – Potato crisps.

Duchesse – Mashed with salt, pepper and grated nutmeg, mixed with butter and egg yolks, shaped like pears, and browned in the oven.

Farcies – Partly boiled, scooped out and filled with truffles, mushrooms, *salpicon* of cooked meat, cooked in the oven.

à la Flamande – Cut into quarters, cooked in consommé with sliced onions and bacon, served with chopped *fines herbes*.

Fondantes – Peeled, egg-shaped, browned in a casserole with a little consommé and butter.

au Four (in the oven) – Washed, baked.

Frites – Cut into square finger shapes.

Galette – Mashed and shaped into small balls then tossed in butter.

Garfield – Cut into large cubes, tossed in butter with *demi-glace* and chopped parsley.

au Gratin – Mashed with egg yolks and butter, sprinkled with breadcrumbs and grated cheese, and browned in the oven.

à la Hongroise – Peeled and cut into quarters, tossed in butter with tomatoes and onions, seasoned with paprika, and stewed in a consommé.

Idéales – Cut into small thin strips, tossed in butter with truffles, shaped into round flat moulds, and baked in the oven.

à l'Impératrice – Baked in their skins, cut in half, scooped out, re-filled, crushed and mixed with butter, cream, egg yolk, and chopped truffles, then browned in the oven.

à l'Impériale – With truffles and artichoke bottoms, tossed lightly in butter, dressed in round flat moulds, and baked in the oven.

à l'Italienne – Sliced, sprinkled with chopped truffles, mushrooms, grated cheese, and chopped salami, then baked in the oven.

au Jus – Boiled, sliced, and stewed in a rich brown stock, sprinkled with parsley.

au Lard – Peeled, quartered, tossed in butter with onions and bacon, stewed in a consommé, and sprinkled with parsley.

en Liards – Small chip potatoes.

Lorette – Mashed, mixed with puff pastry and grated cheese, bound with egg yolk, shaped into sausages, breadcrumbed, and fried.

à la Lyonnaise – Boiled, sliced, mixed with fried onions, and tossed in butter.

Macaire – Baked potatoes, scooped out, pulp mixed with *fines herbes* and butter, then moulded into round cakes, and browned in butter.

Maître d'Hôtel – Boiled, peeled, sliced, cooked in milk and butter with cream, and served with *Maître d'Hôtel* butter.

Marquise – Mashed with yolks of egg and tomato purée, shaped into small round cakes, and baked in the oven.

à la Menthe – New potatoes boiled in salt water with a bunch of fresh mint.

Mignonettes – Small fried potatoes.

Mikado – Large potatoes crinkle-sliced and fried.

Mireille – Peeled, cut into strips, mixed with artichoke bottoms and truffles, and cooked in the oven with butter.

Monselet – New potatoes, sliced in butter, dressed in a dish surrounding sliced truffles and mushrooms mixed with *demi-glacé*.

Mont-Doré – Mashed, mixed with butter and egg yolk, shaped into a pyramid, sprinkled with breadcrumbs and grated cheese, browned in the oven.

Mousseline – Mashed, mixed with egg yolk and whipped cream, shaped into small pears, and browned in the oven.

Natures – Egg-shaped, peeled, boiled in salted water.

au Nid – Egg-shaped soufflé potatoes served in a nest of straw fried potatoes.

Ninette – Peeled, cut into small strips, sprinkled with

grated cheese, and baked in the oven with melted butter poured over.

Noisette – Nut-shaped potatoes either fried or cooked in butter in the oven.

à la Normande – Sliced, tossed in butter with chopped leeks and onions, sprinkled with flour, and stewed in milk.

Paille (straw potatoes) – Peeled, shredded, and fried.

Parisienne – Small, nut-shaped *Noisette* potatoes.

Parmentier – Peeled, cut into cubes, mixed with meat glaze, parsley, and tossed in butter.

Paysanne – Peeled, cut into thick slices, mixed with lean bacon, chopped onions, lettuce, sorrel and garlic, and stewed in a white stock.

Persillées – New, cooked in a consommé with butter. Sprinkled with parsley.

à la Polonaise – Cut into quarters, stewed in butter and cream, served sprinkled with capers.

Pont Neuf – Half-inch-square fried potatoes.

à la Provençale – Sliced, tossed in oil with crushed garlic, and seasoned with parsley.

Purée – Mashed.

Rissolées – Egg-shaped, browned in butter.

en Robe de Chambre – Baked (in their dressing-gowns) in their skins.

Rôties – Roasted.

Sautées – Sliced and tossed lightly in butter, sprinkled with chopped parsley.

à la Savoyarde – Sliced, ranged in layers and covered with grated cheese, garlic-flavoured butter and milk. Cooked in the oven, then browned for a short while after more cheese has been added.

Saxonnes – Mashed, mixed with mashed onions, turnips, egg yolks, and butter, rolled in breadcrumbs and fried.

Schneider – Sliced and stewed in brown stock and butter, sprinkled with *fines herbes*.

Soufflées – Thickly sliced and deep fried till they are soft, allowed to cool, then deep fried again to make them puff up.

Surprise – Baked potatoes that have been scooped out and mixed with butter, grated cheese and cream, re-filled, baked a little longer, and served upside down.

Suzette – Peeled, partly baked in butter, scooped out and filled with the pulp mixed with egg yolk, cream, diced chicken, diced tongue, truffles, and mushrooms. Served on dish paper.

à la Tyrolienne – Boiled new potatoes, sliced, covered with Gruyère shavings and cream sauce, and baked in the oven.

à la Vapeur – Steamed.

à la Viennoise – Sliced new potatoes seasoned with paprika and grated nutmeg and baked in the oven with peeled and chopped tomatoes.

Voisin – Anna potatoes sprinkled with grated cheese.

BIBLIOGRAPHY

A Handbook of Wine, Wm. J. Todd (Cape).

Dictionnaire de Cuisine, J. Favre (Corbeille, 1902).

Guide to Good Food and Wine, André Simon (Collins).

Hors d'œuvre & Cold Table, W. Heptinstall (Faber).

Larousse Gastronomique (Paul Hamlyn).

Modern Culinary Art, H. Pellapart (Comptoir Français du livre, 1935).

Restaurant Service, Crippa & Simms (E.U.P.).

The Whole Art of Dining, J. Rey (Carmona & Baker).

La Cuisine Anglaise et Américaine (1904).

La Grande Cuisine (1902).

La Escargots, Jean Cadart (Lechevalier).

Les Production du Foie Gras, Bernard Vuatrin (Baillière et fils).

Le Guide Culinaire, Escoffier (1907).

Haute Cuisine, Jean Conil (Faber).

INDEX